The Relationship BULLSHIT Men Fall For

What I Learned from Hundreds of Women

Richard Lowe

The Writing King

The Relationship BULLSHIT Men Fall For

Table of Contents

See books by Richard Lowe at

https://masterofworlds.com

Get free publishing insights and industry updates at

https://thewritingking.substack.com

For ghostwriting and book coaching services see

https://thewritingking.com

Disclaimer

I'm not a therapist, psychologist, psychiatrist, counselor, social worker, marriage counselor, or licensed mental health professional of any kind. I have no formal training in psychology, therapy, relationship counseling, or any related field.

Everything in this book is my personal opinion based on my experiences and observations. That's it. This isn't professional advice, medical advice, psychological advice, or therapeutic guidance.

Individual results vary. What works for one person might not work for another. I make no guarantees about the effectiveness of anything discussed in this book.

This book is not intended to diagnose, treat, cure, or prevent any mental health condition or psychological issue. If you're dealing with serious relationship problems, domestic violence, mental health issues, or emotional distress, get help from qualified professionals immediately.

Some content discusses toxic relationships, manipulation, abuse, and other serious topics that may be triggering. You've been warned.

The examples in this book are based on my observations and experiences but don't represent specific individuals. Any resemblance to actual people is coincidental.

This book contains strong language and frank discussions about relationship dynamics that some people may find offensive. If that's you, don't read it.

If you're in immediate danger, contact emergency services (911 in the US) or the National Domestic Violence Hotline (1-800-799-7233).

By reading this book, you acknowledge that you're responsible for your own decisions and actions. Don't blame me if you fuck up your relationships by misapplying this information.

These are my views, not necessarily the views of the publisher or anyone else.

This book is written from a US perspective and primarily addresses relationship dynamics, cultural patterns, and social expectations common in American society. Relationship norms, gender roles, and cultural messaging vary significantly between countries and cultures.

The patterns in this book are common relationship dynamics, not universal rules about all men or women. People are individuals with their own communication styles and needs. Use these insights as guidelines for recognizing potential issues, not as assumptions about everyone you meet.

Preface

I'm not a relationship expert. I'm not a therapist, a pickup artist, or some guru with a system to sell you. I'm just a guy who spent thirty-plus years trying every approach with women and finally figured out what works and what's complete bullshit.

Here's my story.

In my twenties, I was that guy who thought the answer to everything was getting laid as much as possible. I wasn't a smooth operator. I was a shy, introverted computer geek who painted fantasy miniatures, built model kits, and read books.

But I figured out how to pick up women, and I went all-in on that strategy. My stupid ADHD hyper-focused brain at work. Hundreds of them. Different women every week, sometimes several in the same week. I can't remember most of their names or faces because they weren't people to me. This was just something I did because I thought it was the right thing for a man to be doing. At least that's what Playboy and my friends told me.

That phase taught me that what most men think they want isn't what they want. Sex didn't make me happy, confident, or fulfilled. It was just an expensive, time-consuming way to avoid dealing with my own issues. But at least I learned what the player lifestyle delivers versus what desperate guys fantasize it will deliver.

Then I got married. Twelve and a half years to a woman who turned out to be a frigid narcissist with an even more narcissistic son. I thought marriage would solve the emptiness that casual sex couldn't fill. Wrong again. Instead of hundreds of meaningless encounters, I got one long, soul-crushing relationship that taught me how all those relationship patterns play out when you're trapped with someone for years.

The marriage ended when she died after an eight-year chronic illness. Even though she had asthma and lung disease, she wouldn't stop her two-pack a day smoking habit.

I won't pretend I was devastated.

After that, something interesting happened. I became a photographer specializing in women performers: reenactors, models, actresses, belly dancers, and even mermaids. For the first time in my life, I learned how to interact with women without wanting anything from them. No sex, no validation, no relationship drama. Just professional respect and genuine friendship.

I was surrounded by beautiful women every weekend. They invited me to their events, trusted me in their private spaces, and became real friends. Not because I was trying to sleep with them or because they wanted something from me, but because I finally learned to treat them like complete human beings instead of toys or emotional support systems.

That phase taught me what most men never learn: how to be friends with women. How to see them as people instead of obstacles, conquests, or sources of drama. How relationships work when both people respect each other's boundaries, and nobody has a hidden agenda.

For the last twelve years, I haven't given a hoot about women romantically. My life is better without all the complications. I'm not bitter. I'm just done. I've tried every dynamic with women, from casual hookups to marriage to genuine friendship, and I learned what each one costs versus what it delivers.

That complete detachment gives me something most relationship advice lacks: objectivity. I'm not trying to get laid, get married, or get validation from women. I don't need to protect anyone's feelings or advance any agenda. I can tell you exactly what works, what doesn't work, and why most of the advice you've been getting is complete horseshit.

This book isn't about how to get women to like you. It's about understanding the predictable patterns that create conflict between men and women, why those conflicts happen, and what you can do about them.

Sometimes the solution is learning to communicate better. Sometimes it's setting boundaries. Sometimes it's walking away from people who won't meet you halfway.

I will not tell you that women are wonderful creatures who deserve your worship. I'm also not going to tell you they're evil bitches who are out to destroy you. They're people with their own needs, drives, and patterns of behavior. Understanding those patterns and your own is the key to having better relationships or knowing when to avoid them entirely.

Most relationship advice comes from people who are still trying to win the game. This advice comes from someone who played every possible version of the game, figured out the rules, and decided the whole thing wasn't worth the effort. That perspective might be exactly what you need to hear.

You don't have to make the same mistakes I made. You don't have to waste decades learning lessons the hard way. Here's what I discovered about the relationship bullshit men fall for, and what works instead.

Use it or don't. Your choice.

Introduction

How many times have you been told that if you just communicate better, your relationship problems will disappear?

How often have you heard that women want sensitive, understanding men who listen to their feelings?

How's that working out for you?

If you're like most guys, you've tried the sensitive approach and discovered it doesn't work like you were promised. You've probably heard the opposite advice from internet tough guys who tell you to be more alpha and treat women like children. Maybe you tried that too.

I'm guessing neither approach gave you what you wanted.

Both sides are feeding you bullshit. The nice guy advice ignores reality, and the alpha male stuff is mostly fantasy. Besides, who wants a slave?

Meanwhile, you're stuck trying to figure out why your relationships keep following the same frustrating patterns.

Men and women have different needs, and those needs often conflict. Not because anyone is evil, but because we're wired differently. When you understand these conflicts instead of pretending they don't exist, you can make better decisions about which relationships are worth your time.

This book covers fifteen patterns that show up in almost every interaction between men and women. These patterns create predictable conflicts. Some can be managed if both people understand what's happening. Others can't be managed, and you need to know when to walk away.

Most relationship advice pretends these conflicts don't exist or tells you they're your fault for not being understanding enough. Garbage. The conflicts happen because they're built into how men and women operate. Recognizing them doesn't make you a bad person. It makes you informed.

I'm not going to tell you how to get women to like you. I'm not going to promise you'll find your soulmate if you follow my system. I don't have a system, and I'm not selling you hope.

I'll show you patterns I've seen hundreds of times. I'll explain why these patterns happen and what you can do about them. Sometimes the answer is learning to work within the pattern. Sometimes it's walking away from people who won't meet you halfway.

The goal isn't to win or lose with women. The goal is to understand what you're dealing with so you can make choices based on reality instead of wishful thinking.

Ready? Let's start calling out the bullshit.

Notes about the Book Cover

For eight years of my life, I photographed women. Mostly belly and burlesque dancers, models, mermaids, reenactors, and even a few supermodels.

When my wife passed away, I went straight into grief. Even though it was a tough relationship—she was a covert narcissist and became very ill for eight years of our 12½-year marriage—I thought she was my soulmate. I was deeply in love despite emotional, verbal, and mental abuse that went on constantly every single day. Add to that her son, my stepson, was an overt narcissist and the two of them played off each other.

For 12½ years my life became walking on rice paper covered with lilacs and potato chips. The least misstep would lead to emotional abuse, manipulation, tears, and many other manipulation techniques. These included everything from fake illnesses to screaming matches.

She often told me that I needed to be fixed, that there was something wrong with me because of my perfectly normal male desires. What I wanted was a friend, lover, and companion. I don't know what she wanted. She refused to state it.

I could go on for a whole other book, and perhaps I will, about how I survived life for 12½ years in a home with two narcissists playing off each other to my detriment.

When she passed away, I went straight into deep grief. Dangerously deep grief. This was a feeling that I didn't like and I knew that I could hurt myself in any number of ways.

Instead, since I have a functional brain and am more intelligent than most, I decided that I would do something about the grief. I picked up my camera and went on hiking trips. I visited every botanical garden within 250 miles of my house and all of the state and national parks in the southwest United States.

I also visited Renaissance festivals. If you're unfamiliar with those, people dress up in costumes, run little shops, and pretend like they're living in a medieval township. For visitors, there are games, shows, food, shopping, and other attractions.

I found myself attracted to the belly dance shows. There was something about the color, grace, and movement that caused the grief to disappear at least momentarily. During that first year at a Renaissance fair, I must have taken 10 to 20,000 pictures and put them all on a website free for anyone to grab. It didn't take long for the belly dancers and other Renaissance fair people to find them.

One day, I was photographing a belly dance show from a group called Oohjam—traditional belly dancers with long flowing costumes, lots of bells and color, and intricate shows. I was in the back row, center seat, with my telephoto lens busy taking pictures.

A lady named Marjhani approached. She was the leader of the group of dancers, dressed in her majestic flowing traditional Middle Eastern gowns. She was also covered in tattoos and had several piercings.

She sat down next to me, put her arms around me, and gave me a huge hug, which was the last thing I expected. She told me that her dancers loved the photos that I'd put on the internet. They wanted me to continue taking them, and they also wanted to invite me to sit in the front row center seat at every show. She even went so far as to ensure there was a sign that said "Richard Seat" at every show after that.

She brought me behind the scenes and had me meet all the dancers, male and female, and even put a dancer on each side of me who showed me the moves on how to belly dance. This made me super uncomfortable, but I shrugged and went along with it. Marjhani became one of my best friends.

This was the beginning of an 8-year period of my life. During the weekdays, I was busy working my job, sometimes 14 hours a day. On the weekends and late at night, I was either at a Renaissance festival or a belly dance show. Marjhani introduced me to all the big names, and every single one of them reserved a seat for me in the front row center so that I could get some good photos.

I put them all on my website, never charging a penny for any of them, and made them available for the reenactors, dancers, and models to use as they would. The Renaissance fair reenactors made a coffee table book which has quite a few of my pictures inside. So, my photos have been published.

That year, I rented a pirate ship and asked about 25 dancers to perform for my birthday. They all came, dressed in their best outfits, and put on a show for me. Yes, I had 25 belly dancers at the house creating a show just for me. I had it catered from a local restaurant because they were giving me the show at no charge and I felt I had to give back somehow.

This became an annual tradition for the next 8 years, only instead of renting a pirate ship, I rented the Community Center in Monrovia because the number of dancers had gone from 25 to over 200. In fact, in the later years this had grown so much that I had to rent 2 venues—the Community Center on Saturday, and a smaller bar or tavern for Friday.

The picture on the cover was taken by my friend Evangelina, a professional photographer. She posed some of the dancers from that night, the ones who remained after the show was finished, and it came out so good that it became my cover.

My best friend Jannah is the dancer in back, with her hands on the head of a dancer in front of her.

I put this on the cover because I think it shows that men and women can be friends. For those eight years, I photographed about 1,200 belly dance shows and 300 Renaissance festivals, plus other events like WWE pay-per-view wrestling matches (I met the Undertaker), World War 2 reenactments, Civil War battles, and even the first world mermaid beauty pageant in the Silverton hotel in Las Vegas.

Many Renaissance festivals hired me to photograph the events. I sponsored about a dozen belly dance shows, which paid for the venue and any profits were donated to groups who take care of women who've been abused. You know, the ones where they have to escape from an abusive relationship and have nowhere to go.

I hope you enjoy the book and see the significance of the cover.

Part 1: The Bullshit That Happens in Normal Relationships

Chapter 1: Why the Red Pill Approach Doesn't Work

Let me tell you about my friend Jake.

Jake discovered the red pill community when he was 28 and pissed off with his dating life. He'd been rejected by women more times than he could count, and all that "just be yourself" bullshit wasn't getting him laid. He thought that's all he wanted. Sex all the time as much as possible.

The red pill promised him answers. Women are hypergamous creatures who only want alpha males. All women respond to the same tactics. Frame control, amused mastery, and dread game. Learn the system, follow the rules, and you'll get the women who are willing and able.

Jake bought it completely.

He started lifting weights, bought new clothes, and practiced being cocky and aloof.

He memorized conversation techniques and studied "shit tests."

He learned to treat every interaction with women like a chess match he had to win.

It worked. Sort of.

Jake started getting laid more often. He felt like he was finally cracking the code. For about six months, he thought he'd figured out women.

Then it all went to hell.

The problem wasn't that the techniques didn't work. It was what they attracted and what they cost him. Women who responded to the red pill routine weren't women he wanted to be around. They were either damaged enough to be impressed by manipulation tactics or shallow enough to fall for his act.

When Jake finally met a woman he genuinely liked, his red pill programming kicked in. Instead of being himself, he was performing. Instead of connecting with her as a person, he was running a game. The relationship lasted three months before she tired of dating a shallow character instead of a real person.

This is the fundamental problem with the red pill approach: it's based on complete horseshit.

The red pill assumes all women are basically the same and respond to the same triggers. Bullshit. Women are individuals with different needs, backgrounds, and personalities. The techniques that work on insecure 22-year-olds don't work on women who have their shit together. The approach that attracts party girls repels women worth dating.

The red pill also assumes that relationships are war. That women are trying to extract resources while giving as little as possible in return. You need to maintain dominance, or they'll lose respect for you. Your fellow men will see you as a simp, and nothing is worse than that. No man wants to be known as a simp.

This creates a paranoid, exhausting way of life. Every conversation becomes a power struggle. Every interaction requires you to be "on" and in character. You can't relax because relaxing might show weakness. You can't be vulnerable because vulnerability is for pussies.

During my player phase, I learned something the red pill guys miss: the techniques work temporarily on certain types of women, but they don't create the relationships most men want.

When you're manipulating women into sleeping with you, you're not building genuine attraction. You're exploiting insecurities and psychological triggers. The women who fall for this aren't falling for you. They're falling for a performance you can't maintain forever.

Worse, the red pill approach turns you into someone you probably don't want to be. It requires you to suppress empathy, treat women as enemies, and view every interaction through the lens of power and control. That's not happiness. That's sociopathy. And you run into the opposite problem; the women you attract are simps. Who wants to date a controlling prick?

I've known several guys who went down the red-pill rabbit hole. A few became successful with women, but they paid a price, unable to form connections because they'd trained themselves to see manipulation as normal. They couldn't trust women because they assumed all women were trying to screw them over. They couldn't be vulnerable because they'd convinced themselves vulnerability was weakness.

The successful red pill guys I knew were miserable. Sure, they had sex, but they didn't have relationships. They had conquests, but they didn't have friends. They had power, but they didn't have love.

The unsuccessful ones were worse. They tried to implement red pill techniques without understanding them, came across as try-hard and creepy, and got rejected even more than before. Then they blamed women for being hypergamous sluts instead of recognizing that their approach was garbage.

Pick-me women might be fun for a while, but eventually it all becomes trite and boring. Relationships need at least some conflict to prosper.

Women worth dating can smell red-pill techniques from across the room. They've dealt with enough manipulative assholes to recognize the patterns. When you try to run game on them, they don't think you're alpha. They think you're pathetic and trying too hard.

The real problem with the red pill: it confuses correlation with causation.

Yes, confident men are more attractive than insecure men. But the red pill assumes acting confident is the same as being confident. It's not. Real confidence comes from competence, self-knowledge, and experience. Fake confidence comes from following scripts.

Yes, women lose respect for men who are doormats (simps). But the red pill assumes that means you need to be dominant and controlling. Wrong. Women want men who have boundaries and self-respect, not men who treat them like children who need managing.

Yes, some women are attracted to men who dominate. But the red pill turns this into a game where you're always performing needing to be in charge, in control. That's not sustainable in a genuine relationship where you care about the person.

The red pill treats symptoms instead of causes. Instead of helping men become genuinely attractive, it teaches them to fake attractiveness. Instead of addressing the real reasons men struggle with women, it provides shortcuts that create fresh problems.

What's the alternative? Start with yourself.

Become someone worth being with instead of learning tricks to fool women into thinking you're worth being with. Develop real confidence through competence and achievement. Learn to enjoy your own company so you're not desperate for female validation. Build a life that's interesting and fulfilling with or without women in it.

Treat women as individual human beings instead of following a script. Listen to what they want instead of pretending not to care. Be honest about who you are instead of performing a character.

Set boundaries based on your values instead of trying to manipulate women into respecting you. Walk away from people who treat you like shit instead of using dread game to control them.

This approach takes longer than memorizing red-pill techniques. It requires you to do work on yourself instead of learning shortcuts. But it leads to relationships with women who like you for who you are, not women attracted to your performance.

The red pill promises simple answers to complex problems. Life doesn't work that way. Relationships worth having require authenticity, vulnerability, and genuine connection. You can't fake those things forever.

Stop trying to game women and start building a life worth sharing.

Chapter 2: Why the Feminist Approach Doesn't Work

My buddy Tom tried the feminist approach to relationships for three years.

He read all the right books. He attended workshops on toxic masculinity and emotional intelligence. He learned to check his privilege and center women's experiences. He practiced active listening and validated feelings. He became the sensitive, enlightened man that feminist relationship advice promised women wanted.

Tom genuinely believed this crap. He wasn't faking it to get laid. He thought treating women as equals meant putting their needs above his own. He bought all the bullshit about the patriarchy and male toxicity.

He thought being an excellent ally meant never disagreeing with women about anything. To do so would show his hatred towards women. He thought masculinity was a poison that needed to be suppressed. And he bought the idea that he would always be toxic just because he was a man. He even believed that picking the bear in the "would you rather encounter a bear in the woods or a man" was the right thing to do, ignoring the utter stupidity of that premise.

The results were predictable.

Women found him boring. They walked all over him. They used him for emotional support and practical help while fucking men who didn't give a shit about feminist theory. Tom became the reliable friend who fixed their cars and listened to them complain about the assholes they were sleeping with.

After three years of this bullshit, Tom was miserable. He'd followed all the rules and gotten none of the results he wanted. Worse, he'd turned himself into someone he didn't recognize or respect.

The feminist approach to male-female relationships is just as broken as the red pill approach, but in the opposite direction.

Where the red pill tells men to dominate women, feminism tells men to submit. The red pill says women are inferior; feminism says men are inherently flawed. Where the red pill promotes manipulation and servitude, feminism promotes self-denial and outright hostility to anything masculine.

Both approaches ignore reality: men and women have different needs, and those needs sometimes conflict. The feminist solution is to pretend men's needs don't matter or shouldn't exist.

Feminist relationship advice tells men to be more emotional, more communicative, more vulnerable. It assumes that men who struggle with relationships are just defective women who need fixing. It ignores the fact that many traditionally masculine traits are attractive to women.

Tom learned this the hard way.

The more sensitive and accommodating he became, the less women respected him. No relationship survives a lack of respect for long. The more he validated their feelings, the more they treated him like a therapist instead of a potential partner. Who wants to date their therapist? The more he suppressed his masculine instincts, the more boring he became.

Feminist theory assumes that relationship problems stem from patriarchy and male privilege. If men would just stop being sexist assholes, relationships would work perfectly. This is naïve and idealistic bullshit.

Most relationship conflicts aren't about power or oppression. They're about incompatible needs and different communication styles. When a woman wants to talk about her feelings and a man wants to solve the problem, that's not patriarchy. That's biology and psychology.

Feminist relationship advice ignores male psychology completely. It treats masculine traits like competitiveness, independence, and problem-solving as character flaws that need to be overcome. It assumes that men who aren't naturally emotional or communicative are broken.

This creates impossible standards. Men are told to be vulnerable but not weak, emotional but not needy, supportive but not controlling. Any expression of masculine behavior gets labeled as toxic. Any assertion of male needs gets dismissed as selfish.

Tom tried to meet these impossible standards and lost himself.

He became a people-pleaser who was afraid to express his own opinions. He let women make all the decisions in his relationships because he didn't want to be controlling. That would prove he was toxic, right? He suppressed his sexual desires because, God forbid, he didn't want to objectify anyone.

The women in his life sensed his lack of authenticity and lost interest. Nobody wants to date someone who has no backbone or personal boundaries. Women don't want men who are afraid to be men, no matter what they say.

The feminist approach also ignores female psychology. It assumes that women want sensitive, accommodating partners who never challenge them or create any conflict. Some women want this, but most don't.

Most women are attracted to men who have their own opinions, their own goals, and their own boundaries. They want partners, not servants. They want men who can stand up to them when necessary, not men who agree with everything they say.

Modern feminist theory treats any male behavior that women don't like as inherently wrong. If women complain about men being too aggressive, then all aggression is toxic. If women complain about men being emotionally unavailable, then all emotional reserve is unhealthy.

This ignores that some behaviors serve important functions even if they create short-term conflict.

Male competitiveness drives achievement and success. Male independence prevents codependency and resentment. Male problem-solving solves problems, even if it's not what women want to hear in the moment.

Tom discovered this when he tried to support his girlfriend through a work crisis. She wanted to vent about her terrible boss, so he listened and validated her feelings like he'd been taught. For weeks, he offered sympathy and emotional support while she complained about the same problems repeatedly.

Finally, he couldn't take it anymore and suggested she look for a new job. She got pissed and accused him of not understanding her needs. But you know what? She started job hunting the next week and found something better within a month. But she still called him a sexist, privileged asshole.

A feminist approach would say Tom was wrong to offer solutions instead of just listening. Reality says his advice helped her, even though it created temporary conflict.

Feminist relationship advice also creates a victim mentality in women. It teaches them that any relationship problems are the man's fault.

If he's not communicating enough, he's emotionally unavailable. If he wants sex more often than she does, he's objectifying her. If he disagrees with her, he's mansplaining.

This makes it impossible to address relationship issues. Instead of working together to find solutions, couples get stuck in power struggles about who's more oppressed.

Tom experienced this firsthand.

Every disagreement with his girlfriend became a discussion about his male privilege. Every time he expressed a preference, she questioned whether it was influenced by toxic masculinity. Every time he wanted something she didn't want, he was being selfish and demanding.

The relationship became exhausting. Tom spent more time analyzing his motivations and checking his behavior than enjoying his girlfriend's company. He walked on eggshells constantly, afraid that any natural male instinct would be labeled as problematic.

The feminist approach treats masculinity itself as the problem. But masculinity isn't toxic. Certain expressions of masculinity can be toxic, just like certain expressions of femininity can be toxic. The solution isn't to eliminate masculine traits but to express them in healthy ways.

Women need men to be men. They need partners who can provide leadership when necessary, who can handle stress without falling apart, who can make tough decisions without endless processing. These are masculine strengths, not character flaws.

Tom finally figured this out when his relationship ended. His girlfriend left him for a guy who was confident, decisive, and unapologetically masculine. The guy wasn't an asshole, but he also wasn't afraid to disagree with her or assert his own needs.

Tom realized he'd been playing a character that nobody wanted to be around. His attempt to be the perfect feminist ally had made him boring, weak, and fake.

You can have your own opinions without being controlling. You can express your needs without being selfish. You can be masculine without being toxic. You can disagree with women without being sexist.

Equality doesn't mean men and women are identical. It means both people's needs and perspectives matter. It means both people may be authentic without suppressing fundamental aspects of their personalities.

Tom learned to set boundaries based on his values instead of feminist theory. He learned to express his needs directly instead of hoping women would guess what he wanted. He learned to be supportive without being a doormat.

Most importantly, he learned that being a good man doesn't require him to stop being a man.

Feminist relationship advice promises that if men just become more like women, relationships will work better. That's bullshit. Relationships work when both people can be authentic while respecting each other's differences.

Stop trying to be the perfect feminist ally and start being an authentic human being with healthy boundaries and genuine respect for women as individuals.

27

Chapter 3: What Good Cross-Gender Relationships Look Like

If the red pill approach is bullshit and the feminist approach is horseshit, what works?

Let me tell you about my friend Dave and his wife Sarah. They've been married for fifteen years, and they're still happy. Not pretending to be happy on social media, truly happy. They laugh together, they argue sometimes, and they've built a life that works for both.

Dave isn't a red pill alpha or a feminist ally. He's just a guy who figured out how to be married to a woman without losing his mind.

Dave and Sarah understand that they're different people with different needs. Dave needs time alone to recharge after work. Sarah needs to talk about her day and connect emotionally. Instead of fighting about this or trying to change each other, they figured out how to accommodate both needs.

When Dave gets home, he gets thirty minutes to decompress in his garage before dinner. Sarah uses that time to call her sister or catch up on her shows. After dinner, they spend time together talking about their day.

Neither gets everything they want all the time, but both get enough to be satisfied.

Dave doesn't pretend to be someone he's not. He's not emotional or touchy-feely, and he doesn't fake it. Sarah doesn't expect him to be her girlfriend. She has female friends for certain types of conversations.

But Dave also doesn't use his personality as an excuse to be a selfish asshole. When Sarah needs emotional support, he provides it even if it's not his natural strength. When she wants to talk through a problem, he listens even if his instinct is to jump straight to solutions.

Sarah doesn't try to fix Dave or make him more sensitive. She accepts that he shows love through actions instead of words.

When he fixes something around the house or takes care of a problem she's been worried about, she recognizes that as his way of caring for her.

They both have boundaries, and they both respect them.

Dave doesn't expect Sarah to be available for sex whenever he wants it, but Sarah doesn't use sex as a weapon either. They talk about their needs and meet in the middle.

Sarah doesn't expect Dave to read her mind, but Dave doesn't ignore obvious signals either. When Sarah says "fine" in that tone, Dave knows she's not fine, and he asks follow-up questions.

They both take responsibility for their own happiness. Dave doesn't expect Sarah to make him happy, and Sarah doesn't expect Dave to solve all her problems. They're partners who support each other, not codependent messes.

This might sound boring compared to the drama you see in movies. But it works. They've been together for fifteen years; they still enjoy each other's company, and they've built a life together that works.

Compare this to Mark and his girlfriend Jessica. Mark read pickup artist books and tried to maintain frame. Jessica read feminist relationship books and constantly analyzed Mark's behavior for signs of toxic masculinity.

Their relationship was exhausting. Every conversation became a power struggle. Every disagreement turned into a debate about gender roles. They spent more time analyzing their relationship than enjoying it.

Mark was always performing masculinity instead of just being himself. Jessica was always looking for problems instead of appreciating what was working. They broke up after two years of constant conflict.

Good relationships between men and women require a few basic things.

Both people need to be honest about who they are and what they need. This doesn't mean being selfish. It means communicating clearly instead of expecting the other person to guess.

Both people need to accept that the other person is different and that those differences aren't character flaws. Men and women often have different communication styles, different emotional needs, and different ways of showing love. Instead of fighting these differences, successful couples work with them.

Compromise matters, and it goes both ways. Dave doesn't get unlimited alone time, and Sarah doesn't get constant attention. But both get enough to be satisfied.

Each person is responsible for their own emotional wellbeing. You can't expect your partner to make you happy, and you can't blame your partner for your unhappiness.

Choose your battles. Not every disagreement needs to become a relationship crisis. Sometimes it's better to let small things go.

Notice what's missing.

No frame control or dread game. No checking privilege or deconstructing toxic masculinity. No complicated system of rules.

Good relationships are simple. They require two people who like each other, respect each other's differences, and will work together.

This doesn't mean relationships are easy. Dave and Sarah have had tough conversations and periods of adjustment. But they approach problems as partners trying to find solutions instead of enemies trying to win.

They don't expect perfection. Dave sometimes needs more alone time than usual, and Sarah sometimes needs more emotional support than usual. Instead of treating these fluctuations as crises, they adjust.

Most relationship advice makes things more complicated than they need to be. Whether it's red pill theories about alpha behavior or feminist theories about emotional labor, the focus is always on complex systems.

Genuine relationships work when you strip away the bullshit and focus on basic human decency. Treat the other person with respect. Communicate honestly. Be willing to compromise. Take responsibility for your own happiness.

That's it. No system, no ideology, no complicated theories.

The best relationships I've seen are between people who figured out how to be themselves while caring about their partner's wellbeing. They don't try to change each other, and they don't lose themselves in the relationship.

Dave is still the same guy he was when he was single. He still enjoys working on cars, watching sports, and spending time alone. Sarah is still the same woman she was when she was single. She still enjoys talking about feelings, spending time with friends, and planning social activities.

The difference is that they've learned how to integrate their individual needs into a shared life. Dave includes Sarah in his interests when she's genuinely curious, and Sarah gives Dave space when he needs it.

This is what successful relationships look like. Not perfect harmony, but a functional partnership between two people who respect each other's authentic selves.

If you want a relationship like this, stop trying to follow systems and start being honest about who you are and what you need. Find someone who's willing to work with you instead of trying to change you.

It's not as dramatic as the relationship advice industry would have you believe, but it works.

Chapter 4: Jannah My Best Friend

I want to tell you about my friend Jannah. She's the best example I can give you of how friendship between a man and a woman works when both people understand the rules and stick to them.

I met Jannah at a belly dance show in 2006. This was my first time photographing this type of show. I began this activity because I felt depressed and constantly sad because of my wife's passing the year before. Something about the dance, movement, colors, and joy of these shows made me come alive again.

I sat in the front row center with my camera, minding my own business, when she and her friend sat down next to me. We started talking during intermission, and by the end of the show, we were friends.

We goofed around. I think she sensed I was feeling down, so she balanced her sword (most belly dancers have swords to use as props in their performances) on her head, did some belly dance moves, and loudly interrupted the show that was going on at the time. We were so rowdy we almost got kicked out of the show. But she cheered me up!

We weren't the kind of friends where I was secretly hoping to get laid. Not the kind where she was using me for emotional support while dating other guys. We were friends.

This happened because, a few days after the show, during a lunch date, we had a conversation that most men and women never have. We talked about what we wanted from each other.

Jannah made it clear from the beginning that she wasn't interested in anything romantic or sexual. She'd just gotten out of a messy relationship and wasn't looking for another one. She also had five kids and was focused on them, her career, and her bellydancing. I'd lost my wife the year before and wasn't ready for anything serious either.

So, we agreed to be friends. Real friends.

Most guys would have walked away at that point. If there's no possibility of sex, what's the point of being friends with a woman? This is exactly the kind of thinking that keeps men from having genuine relationships with women.

I stuck around because Jannah was interesting. She was smart, funny, and had her own opinions about things. She wasn't looking to me to solve her problems or validate her feelings. She was just a person I enjoyed talking to, photographing, and traveling with.

We started hanging out regularly. Not dates, just friends doing things together. We'd go to shows, Renaissance festivals, check out new restaurants, or just sit and talk about whatever was on our minds.

The key was boundaries. We both knew exactly what the relationship was and what it wasn't. No ambiguity, no hidden agendas, no hoping the other person would change their mind.

When I wanted to take a trip to the Grand Canyon, I asked Jannah if she wanted to come along. Her first reaction was suspicion. Guys rarely invite women on trips without expecting something in return.

I explained that I just wanted company for the trip. I didn't want to go alone, and I thought she'd enjoy seeing the Grand Canyon. We had another conversation about boundaries before we left. I clarified that this was a friendship trip, nothing more.

We took the train from Union Station in Los Angeles to Williams, Arizona, in a sleeper car. She took the top bunk, and I rode in the lower one. Since it was late November, the temperature outside was a frosty 5 degrees. It was an 18-hour trip, so we had plenty of time to eat in the train dining car (the food came with the tickets), talk to people, and get some sleep. Somehow the rocking of the train knocked us both out.

The train stopped for five minutes, leaving us on a concrete pad in the middle of nowhere, with snowflakes in the air. The temperature had dropped to subzero. No worries though, a van arrived within a short time to carry us to Williams. We had a few hours to kill in town, so we ate breakfast, then watched the western shows being performed all over town.

After that, we boarded the historic railway, a steam train that brought us down to the canyon. As part of the entertainment, actors playing bandits rode up to the train and 'robbed' all the passengers, then took a hostage (Jannah, of course) before giving everything back with great fanfare.

We spent three days exploring the park, talking, and just enjoying each other's company. On the first morning, Jannah dressed in her belly dance outfit and did a one-hour performance on the rim of the canyon in 10-degree weather. We gathered a sizable crowd, and I got some great photos of her.

We shared a room at Maswik Lodge with two beds. Never once did either of us try to make it something it wasn't. We were friends on a trip together, and that's exactly what it was.

I had every opportunity to ruin the friendship. But I didn't; in fact, it never even crossed my mind.

That trip taught me something. Friendship with a woman can be just as fulfilling as romantic relationships, sometimes more so. There was no sexual tension, no games, no wondering what the other person was thinking. We could just relax and enjoy each other's company.

After that, we started taking an annual cruise together. There was a belly dance cruise that left from Long Beach and went to Ensenada. About a hundred dancers would go on this cruise every year, taking classes and putting on shows; it was a photographer's dream.

Jannah and I went as roommates. Again, we shared a cabin, and again, it was purely platonic. We both enjoyed the cruise, the shows, and the company of all the other dancers.

We did this for four years in a row. By the third year, Jannah had a boyfriend. He was initially suspicious about her going on a cruise with another man, but Jannah explained our friendship, and he eventually understood that there was nothing romantic between us.

That boyfriend became her husband. Even after they got married, he was fine with our friendship and cruises together because he understood our boundaries were real and had been tested over the years.

This friendship lasted over a decade. We traveled together, spent holidays together, and supported each other through various life changes. I was never tempted to make it into something romantic, and she never used our friendship as a substitute for a genuine relationship.

What made this work?

First, we were both honest about what we wanted. Neither of us was pretending to want friendship while secretly hoping for something else. We genuinely enjoyed each other's company with no ulterior motives.

Second, we respected each other's boundaries. When Jannah said she wasn't interested in romance, I believed her and acted accordingly. When I said I just wanted friendship, she believed me and didn't treat me like a potential boyfriend who needed to be managed.

Third, we both had our own lives. Jannah didn't expect me to be her emotional support system, and I didn't expect her to be mine. We had other friends, other interests, and other sources of fulfillment.

Fourth, we treated each other like equals. I didn't try to fix her problems or tell her how to live her life. She didn't try to change me or make me more sensitive. We accepted each other as we were.

Most men can't have friendships like this because they can't stop thinking about sex. Every interaction with a woman becomes about whether she might be interested in sleeping with them. They can't just enjoy a woman's company without wondering if it might lead to something more.

Most women can't have friendships like this because they're used to men who always have hidden agendas. They assume that any man who wants to spend time with them is just trying to get laid, so they're always on guard.

Jannah and I proved that it's possible for men and women to be genuine friends when both people are honest about their intentions and willing to stick to their boundaries.

This friendship also showed me what I'd been missing in my romantic relationships. The constant sexual tension, the games, the wondering what the other person really wanted, all of that was exhausting. With Jannah, I could just be myself without performing or trying to impress anyone.

I learned women are interesting people when you stop thinking of them as potential sexual partners. Jannah had insights, opinions, and experiences that enriched my life in ways that had nothing to do with romance or sex.

She also showed me that women can be direct and honest when they're not trying to manipulate a romantic situation. There were no hints, no passive-aggressive behavior, no expecting me to read her mind. If she wanted something or had a problem with something, she said so.

This is what friendship between men and women can look like when both people approach it honestly. No games, no hidden agendas, no trying to change the other person into something they're not.

Most relationship advice focuses on romantic relationships and assumes that's the only valuable connection you can have with the opposite sex. Bullshit. Some of the most satisfying relationships I've had with women have been friendships where sex was never part of the equation.

If you want to understand women better, start by learning how to be friends with them. Not fake friends where you're hoping for more, but genuine friends where you appreciate them as people.

This requires you to see women as individuals instead of as a category. It requires you to be honest about your intentions instead of pretending to want friendship while hoping for sex. And it requires you to respect boundaries instead of constantly testing them.

Jannah taught me that friendship between men and women isn't just possible; it can be one of the most rewarding types of relationships you can have. But only if you're willing to be honest, respectful, and genuine about what you want from each other.

Most men miss out on this because they can't get past their own sexual agenda. Their loss.

Chapter 5: The Selective Equality Trap

Derek and Ashley fought about this for months before either of them understood what they were actually fighting about.

It started with dinner. Ashley had been talking about equality since the day they met — equal pay, equal respect, equal standing in every decision they made together. Derek took that seriously. So when she started complaining that he never paid for dinner anymore, he pointed it out. She made more than he did. She'd said herself she wanted to be treated as an equal. He was doing exactly that.

Ashley called him cheap. He called her a hypocrite. She told him he was using equality as an excuse to avoid being a man. He told her she couldn't have it both ways. She brought up the patriarchy. He said that was deflection. They went in circles for weeks, both of them getting angrier, both of them absolutely convinced the other person was being unreasonable.

They almost didn't make it through it. What saved them was that they loved each other enough to keep talking past the point where most couples would have given up.

This is the selective equality trap, and it destroys more relationships than almost any other communication issue. Women want equality in some areas but traditional treatment in others. Men either go full traditional or full equality and get pissed when women want something different depending on the situation.

Ashley genuinely believed in equality. She wanted equal pay, equal respect, equal decision-making power in the relationship. But she also wanted Derek to pay for dinner and open doors for her because those things made her feel cared for and valued.

Derek saw this as hypocritical bullshit. Either you want equality or you don't. Either you can pay your own way and open your own doors, or you want to be treated like you're helpless. Pick one.

Both approaches are wrong because they're trying to apply logic to emotions and social conditioning.

Important distinction: This isn't about gold diggers or women who use dating to get expensive meals, rent money, or luxury items. These women exist, but they're playing a different game. They're using relationships as a financial strategy, not expressing emotional needs.

Ashley wanted Derek to pay for the $30 dinner because it made her feel valued, not because she couldn't afford it or was trying to extract money from him. There's a massive difference between wanting occasional gestures that show care and systematically using men for financial gain.

If a woman expects you to pay for everything, buy her expensive gifts, or cover her living expenses without reciprocating effort or investment in the relationship, that's not selective equality—that's exploitation. The dynamics we're discussing here apply to genuine relationships where both people are invested, not situations where one person is using the other.

Ashley wasn't being hypocritical when she wanted Derek to pay for dinner. She was expressing a desire to feel valued and pursued. The money wasn't the point. The gesture was the point. Derek's refusal to pay felt like a refusal to invest effort in making her feel special.

Derek wasn't being cheap when he stopped paying for everything. He was trying to treat Ashley as an equal partner instead of supporting her financially. His logic was sound, but his execution ignored the emotional component of the gesture.

The selective equality trap happens because equality and emotional connection operate by different rules. Equality is about fairness, logic, and consistent treatment. Emotional connection is about gestures, effort, and making someone feel valued.

Women aren't wrong for wanting both. Men aren't wrong for being confused by the inconsistency. But both sides fuck up when they refuse to understand what the other person needs.

Ashley needed to feel like Derek was willing to invest effort in making her feel special. Derek needed to feel like Ashley appreciated his efforts instead of constantly moving the goalposts about what equality meant.

The solution isn't to abandon equality or to ignore emotional needs. It's to recognize that they're different categories that sometimes overlap and sometimes conflict.

Derek could have paid for dinner occasionally, not because Ashley couldn't afford it, but because he wanted to do something nice for her. Ashley could have appreciated Derek's gesture without making it about gender roles or her ability to pay for herself.

Instead, they turned it into a philosophical debate about consistency and fairness. Derek felt like Ashley was being manipulative. Ashley felt like Derek was being selfish.

This pattern shows up everywhere. Women want equal treatment at work but still want men to be protective in social situations. They want to split household chores equally but still want men to handle certain traditionally masculine tasks. They want emotional support and nurturing but also want to be seen as strong and independent.

Men see these as contradictions because we think in terms of consistent rules and logical frameworks. Women see these as different needs in different contexts because they think in terms of emotional connection and social dynamics.

Neither approach is wrong, but they're incompatible when both people insist their way is the only valid way.

The selective equality trap isn't really about equality. It's about the difference between treating someone fairly and making them feel valued. Sometimes those things align, and sometimes they don't.

What finally broke through for Derek was a conversation where Ashley stopped talking about equality and just told him the truth: when he stopped paying for dinner, it felt like he'd stopped trying. Like she'd already been won and he'd moved on to other things. The money was never the point. The effort was. He'd been so focused on the logic of equal treatment that he'd missed what she was actually asking for.

What broke through for Ashley was harder. She had to admit that she'd been using feminist framing as armor in arguments she didn't know how to have directly. Derek wasn't the patriarchy. He was her boyfriend trying to figure out what she wanted, and she kept moving the target and then getting angry when he missed. That was on her.

The key is separating equality from emotional connection. You can treat someone as an equal while still doing things that make them feel special. You can want equal treatment in most areas while still appreciating traditional gestures in others.

But you can't use equality as a weapon when it benefits you and then abandon it when it doesn't. And you can't use logic to dismiss someone's emotional needs just because they seem inconsistent.

Women aren't wrong for wanting both equality and special treatment. Men aren't wrong for being confused by what seems like moving goalposts. But both sides are wrong when they refuse to understand that different situations call for different approaches.

Relationships aren't about philosophical consistency. They're about understanding what your partner needs and meeting those needs without abandoning your own values.

Chapter 6: The Hint and Hope Pattern

Rachel wanted to go to her company's holiday party with her boyfriend Mike, but she didn't want to ask him directly. Instead, she mentioned how nice the venue was going to be, talked about how her coworkers were bringing their partners, and complained about how boring work events usually were without someone to talk to.

Mike heard her comments but didn't pick up on what she was really asking for. When Rachel showed up at the party alone and spent the evening pissed off, Mike was confused as hell. He had no idea she'd wanted him to come with her.

"Why didn't you just ask me to go?" Mike said when Rachel finally explained why she was upset.

"I shouldn't have to ask," Rachel replied. "You should have known I wanted you there."

I lived this for twelve and a half years with my wife Claudia. She was the master of hints. She'd drop subtle signals about everything — what she wanted for dinner, what she needed around the house, how she was feeling, what she expected from me that day. I missed every single one of them. Not because I didn't care. Because I don't operate that way. I want things stated plainly. Just tell me what you want. That was apparently too much to ask.

This is the hint and hope pattern, and it causes more fights than almost any other communication style. Women drop hints about what they want, and hope men will pick up on them. Men miss the hints because they're not looking for subtext. Both sides end up frustrated and resentful.

Rachel thought her hints were obvious. She'd mentioned the party multiple times, talked about other couples going, and made it clear she didn't want to go alone. From her perspective, Mike should have offered to come with her.

Mike heard her comments as information, not requests. She was telling him about her work party, not asking him to attend. He didn't offer to come because he didn't realize she wanted him there.

This pattern happens because women often communicate indirectly to avoid appearing demanding or needy. They drop hints and hope their partner will pick up on what they want. Men communicate directly and expect the same in return. They take words at face value instead of looking for hidden meanings.

Rachel's hints made perfect sense to her because that's how she communicated with her female friends. When women talk to each other about problems or desires, they expect the listener to read between the lines and offer help or support without being directly asked.

Mike's literal interpretation made perfect sense to him because that's how he communicated with everyone. When he wanted something, he asked for it directly. When someone told him information, he processed it as information, not as a request for action.

Neither approach is wrong, but they're incompatible when people refuse to adjust their communication style.

The hint and hope pattern creates problems because it sets up situations where one person has expectations that the other person doesn't know about. Rachel expected Mike to attend her work party. Mike didn't realize he was expected to do anything.

When the expectation isn't met, the person who dropped the hint feels ignored or uncared for. The person who missed the hint feels blindsided and confused.

Rachel felt like Mike didn't care about her needs because he didn't offer to come to the party. Mike felt like Rachel was being unfair because she never asked him to come. They were both right from their own perspectives.

The problem with hints is that they require mind-reading. Rachel assumed Mike would understand what she wanted based on context and subtext. Mike assumed Rachel would tell him directly if she wanted something from him.

Women often hint instead of asking directly because they've been taught that being too direct makes them seem pushy or demanding. They want their partners to offer help or support voluntarily, which feels more caring than having to ask for it.

Men often miss hints because they're not looking for them. We process communication literally and assume that if someone wants something from us, they'll ask for it directly.

The hint and hope pattern also shows up in household management. Women will mention that the kitchen is messy, hoping their companion will offer to clean it. Men hear the comment as an observation, not a request for help.

Women will talk about being stressed about an upcoming deadline, hoping their partners will offer to take on more household responsibilities. Men hear the comment as information sharing, not a request for support.

The solution isn't for women to stop hinting or for men to become mind readers. It's for both sides to understand how the other person communicates and adjust accordingly.

Rachel could have asked Mike directly to come to her work party instead of hoping he'd figure it out from her hints. Mike could have learned to recognize when Rachel's comments were requests for support or action.

But this requires both people to step outside their natural communication styles and meet in the middle.

Rachel eventually learned to be more direct about what she wanted from Mike. Instead of hinting that she needed help with something, she'd ask for it. Instead of hoping Mike would offer to do things, she'd request them clearly.

Mike learned to listen for subtext in Rachel's comments and ask clarifying questions when he wasn't sure what she needed. Instead of taking everything at face value, he'd ask, "Are you telling me this because you want me to do something about it?"

The hint and hope pattern isn't really about communication style. It's about different expectations for how people should anticipate and meet each other's needs. Women often want their needs to be anticipated. Men often want their partners to state their needs clearly.

Both approaches have merit, but they only work when both people are using the same communication framework. Mixing hint-based communication with literal interpretation creates misunderstandings that neither side saw coming.

Chapter 7: Stress Management Styles

Here's something I watched happen dozens of times in the belly dance world, always the same way.

Show ends. Two hours of performing, hundreds of people, music, energy, chaos. The dancers come offstage buzzing. They want to talk, decompress out loud, replay the night, laugh about what went wrong and what went right. The whole drive home is a full debrief. They need to get it out.

Their husbands and boyfriends — the ones who'd been there all night hauling equipment and running sound and standing in the back — they go quiet. Not cold, not checked out. Just quiet. They needed the noise to stop for a while before they had anything to say.

Both people had just survived the same evening. Both were processing it. They just processed in completely opposite directions, and if neither one understood that about the other, the drive home became a fight about nothing.

This is the fundamental difference in how men and women handle stress, and it causes more relationship conflicts than people realize. Women process stress externally through talking and social connection. Men process stress internally through isolation and mental space.

Lisa needed to talk through her stress to make sense of it. The act of verbalizing what happened helped her organize her thoughts, validate her feelings, and figure out how to handle similar situations in the future. Talking wasn't making her stress worse. It was how she worked through it.

Matt needed quiet time to process his stress before he could articulate it to anyone else. He had to sort through his emotions internally before he was ready to discuss them externally. Isolation wasn't avoidance. It was preparation for engagement.

When Lisa came home upset and immediately started talking, Matt felt overwhelmed and pressured to respond before he'd had time to process his own day. When Matt came home and went quiet, Lisa felt shut out and worried that he was angry with her or dealing with something serious.

Neither of them understood that the other person's stress management style was legitimate and necessary.

Lisa interpreted Matt's need for quiet time as rejection. She thought if he really cared about her, he'd want to hear about her day and share what was going on with him. His withdrawal felt like emotional abandonment.

Matt interpreted Lisa's immediate need to talk as demanding and inconsiderate. He thought if she really cared about him, she'd give him time to decompress before launching into a detailed analysis of her workday. Her intensity felt overwhelming.

Both reactions made sense from their own perspectives, but they were based on fundamentally different approaches to stress management.

Women often need to move their bodies, connect with friends, or engage in social activities when they're stressed. They need external stimulation and interaction to work through their emotions.

Men often need physical space, mental tasks, or solitary activities when they're stressed. They need to withdraw from external demands to figure out their internal state.

Neither style is superior. They're just different approaches to the same goal: managing stress and returning to emotional equilibrium.

The problem comes when people assume their partner's stress management style is wrong or unhealthy. Lisa thought Matt was emotionally unavailable. Matt thought Lisa was codependent and anxious.

Lisa was using her natural stress management tools, and Matt was using his. Both approaches worked for the people using them, but they clashed when both people were stressed at the same time.

The solution isn't for one person to abandon their natural stress management style. It's for both people to understand and accommodate each other's needs without taking them personally.

Lisa learned that Matt's need for quiet time wasn't about her or their relationship. It was about his process for managing stress. She could still process her own stress externally without requiring Matt to be her primary audience when he was also dealing with his own shit.

Matt learned that Lisa's need to talk through her stress wasn't about being dramatic or attention-seeking. It was about her process for making sense of difficult situations. He could give her space to process without feeling responsible for solving her problems.

They developed a system where Lisa would process her stress with friends or family when Matt needed quiet time, and Matt would engage with Lisa's processing when he'd had time to decompress from his own day.

This required both to stop judging the other person's stress management style and to start accommodating it.

The stress management difference also shows up in how people handle relationship conflicts. Women often want to talk through problems immediately when they arise. Men often need time to think about the situation before they're ready to discuss it productively.

Women interpret men's request for processing time as avoidance or lack of caring. Men interpret women's demand for immediate discussion as pressure and impatience.

Both reactions are understandable, but they're based on different assumptions about how emotional processing works.

This doesn't mean accepting bad behavior. If someone uses their processing style as an excuse to avoid responsibility or tough conversations, that's a problem. But most people are genuinely trying to manage their stress in the way that works best for them.

The key is recognizing that different people have different needs when they're overwhelmed, and those needs aren't personal attacks on you or your relationship.

Chapter 8: The Space vs. Togetherness Gap

I knew a belly dancer named Aylin. Turkish, incredibly talented, and the most relentless social engine I've ever seen in my life. The woman didn't have an off switch. After performing for two hours straight, she'd be the last person on the floor at the after-party, still going, still talking to everyone, feeding off the crowd like it was oxygen.

Her husband Greg was the opposite. Quiet guy, showed up to her shows, carried equipment, stood off to the side with a beer and a patient smile. He was proud of her. Supported everything she did. Just didn't need to be in the middle of it.

I think they eventually divorced.

I'm not surprised. Not because anything was wrong with either of them, but because that gap — one person who gains energy from constant social connection and one person who needs space and quiet to function — is one of the hardest incompatibilities to bridge. Most couples never even figure out that's what they're fighting about. They just know something feels off, and they both blame each other for it.

Aylin probably felt like Greg was dragging her down. Like he didn't understand her world or didn't want to. Greg probably felt like he was always being pulled somewhere he didn't want to be, or silently judged for wanting to go home.

Neither of them was wrong. They just needed completely different things to feel like themselves.

This shows up two ways in relationships, and they're really the same problem wearing different clothes.

The first version is the social calendar fight. One person wants to go out — happy hours, parties, dinners with friends, events on weekends. The other person wants to stay home, recharge, keep the social obligations minimal. The extrovert reads the introvert's reluctance as antisocial, boring, or a sign they don't care about sharing a life. The introvert reads the extrovert's constant need to be out as exhausting, superficial, or a sign they can't just be content with what they have at home.

The second version is the togetherness fight. One person wants to do everything together — share every plan, check in before making commitments, build their life around the relationship. The other person needs independent time, separate friendships, space to exist as an individual. The high-connection person reads the autonomous person as pulling away or not invested. The autonomous person reads the high-connection person as clingy or controlling.

Same root, different branch. One person needs more. The other needs less. Both think their amount is normal.

The mistake both sides make is assuming their baseline is the right one.

If you're wired like Aylin, being around people isn't a choice — it's how you process the world. Solitude doesn't restore you. It makes you restless and anxious. When Greg wanted a quiet night in after a show, it probably felt to her like being asked to hold still when everything in her wanted to move.

If you're wired like Greg, crowds and constant social obligation don't energize you — they drain you. After a full weekend of events, being around people, even people he liked, cost him something. He needed quiet to get it back. Aylin's need to keep going probably felt relentless.

Both of those experiences are real. Neither person is being difficult. They're just built differently.

The problem isn't the difference itself. It's when each person decides the other one needs to change.

Extroverts push. They think if their partner just tried harder, got out more, stopped being so antisocial, they'd discover they actually like it. Introverts dig in. They think if their partner just calmed down, stopped needing so much stimulation, learned to appreciate a quiet life, everyone would be happier.

Both are trying to fix something that isn't broken.

The couples who make it work don't convert each other. They negotiate. The extrovert pursues some of their social life independently — friends, events, the after-party — without requiring their partner to come to everything. The introvert shows up for the things that actually matter to their partner without treating every invitation like an ambush.

Neither gets everything they want. Both get enough to stay sane.

The autonomy side of this is worth being direct about. Some people experience love as closeness — the more intertwined your lives, the more secure they feel. Other people experience love as choosing each other while staying whole — two separate people who share a life without merging into one. Neither model is wrong. But when a high-connection person is with a high-autonomy person, the connection person often reads independence as rejection, and the autonomy person reads connection needs as control.

She's not clingy. She's wired to feel loved through togetherness. He's not pulling away. He's wired to feel healthy through independence.

When you understand that, you stop taking it personally. You start figuring out how to give each other enough of what you need without bleeding the other person dry.

If you're the introvert or the autonomous one — show up more than feels natural sometimes. It costs you less than you think, and it means more than you realize.

If you're the extrovert or the high-connection one — build a life that doesn't depend entirely on your partner to fill it. Friends, community, outlets that are yours. It takes pressure off the relationship and it keeps you from resenting someone for being who they are.

Greg probably wasn't going to become the guy dancing until 2am. Aylin probably wasn't going to become someone who wanted a quiet life.

The question was always whether there was enough middle ground. Sometimes there isn't. But most people never even find out because they spend all their energy trying to change each other instead of figuring out whether they can work with what's actually there.

Chapter 9: Action vs. Process Preferences

She booked the vacation after three weeks of research. He canceled the restaurant reservation she'd spent twenty minutes choosing and picked somewhere else on the spot because the reviews looked fine to him.

Neither told the other one before doing it. Neither thought they needed to.

This is what action versus process looks like when it collides — two people with completely different default speeds, both convinced their approach is just common sense. The action person can't understand why anyone would spend three weeks planning a trip that takes three days. The process person can't understand why anyone would hand money to the first restaurant that popped up on a search.

They're not arguing about vacations or restaurants. They're arguing about how decisions should be made, and neither one has ever stopped to question whether their way is the only sensible way.

This is the action versus process preference divide, and it shows up in almost every decision couples and friends must make together.

Tyler preferred immediate action when faced with problems. He wanted to identify the issue, find a solution, and implement it as quickly as possible. Extended discussion and analysis felt like wasted time when he could take steps to fix the problem.

Jessica preferred a thorough process when faced with decisions. She wanted to gather information, consider alternatives, and think through the implications before committing to a course of action. Quick decisions felt reckless and likely to create bigger problems later.

Neither approach was wrong, but they were incompatible when both people insisted their way was the only sensible approach.

Tyler's action-oriented approach worked well for straightforward problems with clear solutions. When something was broken, you fixed it. When something needed to be done, you did it. Overthinking simple issues just delayed the inevitable and created unnecessary stress.

Jessica's process-oriented approach worked well for complex decisions with long-term consequences. When multiple factors needed to be considered, rushing into action often created more problems than it solved. Thinking things through prevented costly mistakes and regrets.

I saw this in my own marriage. Claudia was the ultimate in putting things off — overthinking every decision, weighing every angle, circling back to the same questions she'd already considered. Me? I'd wake up on a Saturday morning with no plan, decide we were going somewhere, and have us packed and in the car within the hour. She'd still be making a list of reasons we should have planned this better. We drove each other insane.

The conflict arose because both people applied their preferred approach to every situation, regardless of whether it was appropriate.

Tyler wanted to use his action approach for car repair, house hunting, vacation planning, and choosing a restaurant for dinner. Jessica wanted to use her process approach for all the same decisions, including ones that didn't require extensive analysis.

When Jessica insisted on researching mechanics for three days before making an appointment, Tyler felt like she was being unnecessarily complicated about a simple car repair. When Tyler wanted to book the first vacation package they found online, Jessica felt like he wasn't taking their financial situation seriously enough.

Both reactions made sense from their own decision-making perspective, but they ignored the reality that different situations call for different approaches.

Some decisions need immediate action. If the car is making a dangerous noise, waiting three days to research mechanics could create a safety hazard. If a good deal on vacation packages expires tomorrow, extensive research might mean missing the opportunity entirely.

Some decisions require careful consideration. Choosing a mortgage, picking a neighborhood to live in, or making major financial commitments shouldn't be rushed just because someone prefers quick action.

The problem wasn't that Tyler and Jessica had different decision-making styles. The problem was that neither of them could recognize when their preferred style was inappropriate for the situation at hand.

Tyler learned to slow down his decision-making process for major choices that would affect them both long-term. Jessica learned to speed up her decision-making process for minor issues that didn't require extensive analysis.

But this required them to step outside their comfort zones and trust that sometimes the other person's approach was more appropriate.

The action versus process divide also shows up in how people handle relationship problems. Action-oriented people want to identify the issue and fix it immediately. Process-oriented people want to explore the underlying dynamics and understand why the problem occurred.

When Tyler and Jessica had a fight, Tyler wanted to apologize, make up, and move on. Jessica wanted to talk through what had happened, understand why they'd miscommunicated, and figure out how to prevent similar conflicts in the future.

Tyler interpreted Jessica's desire for extended discussion as dwelling on negative shit and making problems bigger than they needed to be. Jessica interpreted Tyler's desire to move on quickly as avoiding the genuine issues and ensuring they'd have the same fight again later.

Both interpretations had merit in different situations.

Sometimes relationship problems are simple misunderstandings that can be resolved with a simple apology and commitment to do better. Sometimes relationship problems are symptoms of deeper communication patterns that need to be addressed before they escalate.

The key is matching the approach to the situation instead of always defaulting to your preferred style.

Chapter 10: Appreciation Language Differences

Marcus spent every weekend doing things for his girlfriend Claire. He'd wash her car, fix things around her apartment, run errands for her, and handle all the practical shit she didn't want to deal with. Claire rarely thanked him for any of it, which pissed him off because he was busting his ass to make her life easier.

Claire spent time every day telling Marcus how much she appreciated him. She'd text him sweet messages, tell him she loved him, compliment his efforts, and verbally acknowledge all the things he did for her. Marcus barely responded to any of it, which pissed her off because she was constantly expressing gratitude and affection.

Each felt unappreciated although they both were actively trying to show appreciation. They were just speaking different languages.

This is the appreciation language difference, and it causes more relationship resentment than people realize. Some people show appreciation through actions. Some people show appreciation through words. When these two types get together, both people end up feeling like their efforts aren't being recognized.

Marcus showed appreciation by doing things. When he cared about someone, he showed it through helpful actions, practical support, and solving problems. He figured if he was washing Claire's car every weekend, it was obvious that he valued her and their relationship.

Claire showed appreciation by saying things. When she cared about someone, she expressed it through verbal affirmation, compliments, and emotional support. She figured if she was telling Marcus she loved him every day, it was obvious that she valued him and their relationship.

Both approaches were valid ways of expressing appreciation, but neither person recognized nor valued the other person's approach.

Marcus interpreted Claire's lack of verbal response to his actions as ingratitude. He thought if she really appreciated what he was doing for her, she'd thank him more often and acknowledge his efforts. Her casual acceptance of his help felt like she was taking him for granted.

Claire interpreted Marcus's lack of verbal response to her words as indifference. She thought if he really appreciated her expressions of love, he'd respond with similar warmth and enthusiasm. His brief replies to her sweet messages made her feel like he didn't care about her feelings.

Neither of them was right about the other person's level of appreciation. They were both appreciative. They just expressed it differently and valued different types of appreciation in return.

The actions versus words divide shows up in friendships too. Some people show they care about friends by being helpful, reliable, and available when needed. Other people show they care about friends by being emotionally supportive, encouraging, and verbally affectionate.

Action-oriented people feel appreciated when others do things for them, help them solve problems, or show up when they need practical support. Words-oriented people feel appreciated when others express gratitude, give compliments, or acknowledge their efforts verbally.

When action people and words people become friends, both sides often feel like the other person doesn't really care about them.

Marcus felt unappreciated because Claire didn't thank him enough for all the practical things he did for her. Claire felt unappreciated because Marcus didn't respond enthusiastically to her verbal expressions of love and gratitude.

I ran into this with Claudia. She loved receiving romantic gifts and gestures — flowers, surprises, that kind of thing. And she'd tell me she loved me, hold hands, say the words. That seemed to be enough for her. For me it wasn't. I'm an action person. I wanted her to initiate — sex, gestures, anything that showed she was thinking about me without being prompted. She never did. I tried explaining what I needed. She refused to change. We were both expressing something, but neither of us was receiving what we actually needed.

The problem wasn't that either person was unappreciative. The problem was that they were looking for appreciation in their preferred language while giving appreciation in their preferred language.

Marcus needed to hear Claire say, "thank you" and acknowledge his efforts verbally. Claire needed to hear Marcus say, "I love you too" and respond to her emotional expressions with similar warmth.

But Marcus was showing appreciation through actions and expecting Claire to show appreciation through actions. Claire was showing appreciation through words and expecting Marcus to show appreciation through words.

They were giving what they wanted to receive instead of giving what the other person wanted to receive.

Marcus learned to respond verbally to Claire's expressions of love and gratitude. When she texted him sweet messages, he texted back with equal warmth. When she told him she appreciated something he'd done, he thanked her for saying so and told her it meant a lot to him.

Claire learned to acknowledge Marcus's actions verbally and show appreciation through actions occasionally. When he washed her car, she thanked him for taking care of her and told him how much his help meant to her. She also started doing practical things for him to show she cared.

They had to step outside their natural appreciation style and learn to speak the other person's language. That's it. Figure out which language the other person speaks, and use it.

Chapter 11: Sex, Frequency, and the Identity Trap

When I was dating Claudia, sex was never an issue. Every date ended the same way. She was enthusiastic, physical, and seemed to genuinely want it as much as I did. I figured I'd finally found someone I was truly compatible with. I married her.

The day after the honeymoon, she turned off like a switch.

Not gradually. Not after a stressful period. Overnight. I spent months trying to figure out what I'd done wrong, what had changed, whether there was something wrong with me. I pushed. I asked. I backed off. I tried being more romantic, more attentive, more patient. Nothing moved the needle.

Finally I asked her directly. She told me the truth, flat out: she'd found her man, she didn't need sex anymore, and it wasn't useful to her.

That's a brutal thing to hear. It's also clarifying. Claudia wasn't broken. She wasn't depressed. She'd used sex to land the relationship she wanted and had no further interest in it once she had me. I hadn't done anything wrong. I'd just married someone for whom sex was a means to an end rather than something she actually wanted.

When I tried to talk about it, she turned vicious. Arguments that went nowhere except to leave me feeling like I was the problem for wanting a normal sex life. She was a narcissist — something I didn't have the vocabulary for at the time — and she was very good at making my needs seem like character defects.

So I went to therapy. Hundreds of hours. I was trying to fix whatever was wrong with me that was causing the problem. She came to couples therapy too, briefly, and used it as a demolition opportunity. She didn't have a problem, after all. Why was she even there? She'd sit across from the therapist and systematically dismantle me while I watched.

The therapy didn't solve anything. Of course it didn't. Because the problem wasn't me.

She emasculated me thoroughly and I believed her. Believed that my desire was excessive, that I was asking for too much, that a reasonable man would just accept the situation and stop making everything about sex. I internalized that for twelve and a half years. And even now, twenty years after she died, that pain is still there. That's how deep that kind of damage goes when it's sustained long enough.

I'm telling you this because the standard advice on mismatched sexual frequency is useless. Communicate more. Find compromise. Be patient. Show her you care about her as a person, not just sexually. I did all of it. None of it touched the actual problem, which was that she didn't want sex and didn't think that was her problem to solve.

Here's what I should have done: left.

Not after a year of trying. Not after hundreds of hours of solo therapy. Early. When the pattern became clear and she made it obvious she had no interest in changing it, I should have recognized that as fundamental incompatibility and walked away. Instead I stayed for over a decade and paid for it with a piece of myself I never fully got back.

Men cannot just turn sex off. This isn't a character flaw or a failure of emotional maturity. It's biology. A man in a sexless marriage isn't going to meditate his way to contentment. He's going to suffer quietly, or act out, or slowly lose himself the way I did. The idea that the solution is to work on yourself until the desire goes away, or until you've become sensitive enough that she'll want you again (and as a side note — women say they want sensitive men, but in my observation it turns most of them off big time), is a lie that keeps men trapped in situations that are genuinely damaging them.

The second problem layered on top of this is that most men — and I was absolutely one of them — tie their sense of worth as a man to whether their partner wants them sexually. When she stopped wanting me, I didn't just feel unloved. I felt like I'd failed as a man. That made me vulnerable to exactly the kind of manipulation my wife was running. She told me the problem was mine and I believed her because some part of me had already decided that her rejection was a verdict on my worth.

It wasn't. Her behavior was about her — her coldness, her narcissism, her willingness to use sex as a tool and then put it away when it had served its purpose. But I couldn't see that clearly because I was too busy trying to fix myself into someone she'd want.

If you're in a relationship where sex has dried up and your partner refuses to acknowledge it as a shared problem — not a rough patch, not a stressful period, but a flat refusal to engage — stop going to therapy alone. Stop trying to become someone different. Start asking whether this is a relationship you should be in at all.

That's not giving up. That's being honest about what a relationship requires to function. For most men sex is vital to a relationship. It confirms their masculinity and that their partner actually desires them. A partner who weaponizes its absence, who uses your desire against you, who watches you suffer and tells you it's your fault — that person isn't someone you can build a life with, no matter how much therapy you do.

I know this from twelve and a half years of trying.

Chapter 12: Visual vs. Emotional Processing

Men and women are not attracted to the same things in the same way, and pretending otherwise creates problems that blindside both people.

Here's the short version: most men are wired to experience attraction visually first. Appearance, physical presence, how someone looks in a specific moment — these things land first and fast. It's not shallow. It's how male attraction actually works at a neurological level.

Most women are wired to experience attraction emotionally first. How a man makes her feel, whether she feels safe and seen and valued — these things drive desire more than appearance. A man she finds physically average can become deeply attractive when he shows up for her consistently. A man she initially found attractive can become completely unappealing if he makes her feel bad about herself.

When these two wiring patterns meet in a relationship and neither person understands the other's, you get a very specific and painful cycle. She gains weight during a stressful period and he pulls back physically without saying why. He pulls back, so she feels judged and unloved, and her attraction to him drops. His withdrawal confirms her fear that she's not enough. Her coldness confirms his feeling that the physical connection is gone. Nobody started a fight. Both people feel like the other person changed.

This is the visual versus emotional processing divide, and it affects how men and women experience attraction, connection, and sexual desire.

Mark processed attraction primarily through visual and physical cues. He was drawn to Lisa's appearance, responded to visual stimulation, and felt sexual desire when she looked attractive to him. This wasn't shallow or superficial. It was how his brain was wired to experience attraction.

Lisa processed attraction primarily through emotional and relational cues. She was drawn to Mark's personality, responded to emotional connection, and felt sexual desire when she felt emotionally close to him. This wasn't prudish or complicated. It was how her brain was wired to experience attraction.

Both approaches were valid ways of experiencing attraction, but they created problems when neither person understood the other's processing style.

Mark didn't understand why Lisa's attraction seemed to disappear when he was less emotionally available. He thought if she found him physically attractive, she should want sex regardless of their emotional connection. Her need for emotional intimacy before physical intimacy felt like unnecessary bullshit.

Lisa didn't understand why Mark's attraction seemed to fluctuate based on her appearance. She thought if he really loved her, he should find her attractive regardless of temporary physical changes. His focus on visual aspects made it feel like he didn't care about her as a person.

Both interpretations missed how the other person naturally processed attraction and desire.

When Mark was less attracted to Lisa because of her weight gain, he thought this was a normal response to physical changes. When Lisa was less attracted to Mark because he made her feel bad about her appearance, she thought this was a normal response to emotional disconnection.

Neither of them could see that their partner's decreased attraction was a predictable response to having their primary attraction triggers disrupted.

Mark's visual processing wasn't about being shallow or caring only about appearance. Physical attraction was how he experienced desire and connection. When that was disrupted, his overall interest in intimacy decreased.

Lisa's emotional processing wasn't about being high-maintenance or needy. Emotional connection was how she experienced desire and attraction. When that was disrupted, her overall interest in intimacy disappeared.

The problem came when they took the other person's attraction style personally instead of understanding it as a different way of processing desire.

Mark felt like Lisa was punishing him for having normal male sexual responses. Lisa felt like Mark was punishing her for normal human weight fluctuations.

Both reactions were based on misunderstanding how the other person experienced attraction.

Mark learned that Lisa's emotional attraction needs weren't about being difficult or complicated. Emotional connection was a prerequisite for her sexual interest. He could maintain emotional intimacy even during periods when he was less visually attracted, which kept their overall connection strong.

Lisa learned that Mark's visual attraction responses weren't about being shallow or judgmental. Physical attraction was how he experienced desire. She could understand his responses without taking them as personal rejection and work on maintaining her physical health for both of their benefits.

They found ways to maintain both emotional and physical connection even when one person's primary attraction triggers were temporarily disrupted.

This required them to stop judging the other person's attraction style and start accommodating it.

The visual versus emotional processing difference also affects how people interpret flirting and attention from others. Visual processors notice when their partner pays attention to attractive people. Emotional processors notice when their partner forms emotional connections with others.

Mark would get jealous when other men looked at Lisa or when Lisa dressed attractively around other people. Lisa would get jealous when Mark had deep conversations with female coworkers or seemed emotionally engaged with other women.

Both types of jealousy were based on understanding their own attraction triggers and assuming their partner worked the same way.

None of this means accepting behavior that crosses relationship boundaries. It means recognizing that different people experience attraction and connection differently, and those differences affect what feels threatening or reassuring in relationships.

Chapter 13: Emotional Labor Expectations

Alex expected his girlfriend Megan to manage the emotional climate of their relationship.

When he was stressed about work, Megan would ask what was wrong and help him process his feelings. When they had a disagreement, Megan would initiate the conversation to resolve it. When Alex's family visited, Megan would handle the social coordination and make sure everyone felt welcome.

Megan was exhausted from being the emotional manager of their relationship. She felt responsible for Alex's moods, their communication, and the overall health of their connection. When Megan was stressed, Alex would wait for her to get over it instead of offering support. When she needed to talk through problems, Alex would listen passively without engaging actively in solutions.

This is the emotional labor expectation gap, and it creates resentment that builds over time until relationships implode.

Alex had learned that women were naturally better at handling emotions and relationships. He thought Megan enjoyed taking care of the emotional side of their partnership because she was good at it. He contributed financially and practically to their relationship, which he thought was his primary responsibility as a man.

Megan had learned that maintaining relationships was largely a woman's responsibility. She thought Alex's emotional passivity was normal male behavior and that she needed to compensate for it by working harder on their connection. She managed their social calendar, remembered important dates, and monitored their relationship health.

Both were operating under bullshit assumptions about gender roles that made their relationship unsustainable.

The emotional labor divide isn't about women being more emotional than men. It's about who takes responsibility for managing emotions, communication, and relationship maintenance.

Alex didn't lack emotional capacity. He could be supportive, start tough conversations, and pay attention to relationship dynamics. He just didn't think those things were his job.

Megan didn't enjoy being the relationship manager. She could let Alex handle his own emotions and expected him to contribute equally to their communication. She just didn't think it was acceptable to stop managing everything.

The problem was their assumption that emotional labor was naturally women's work instead of something both partners should share.

When Alex was having a bad day, he'd come home and wait for Megan to notice, ask what was wrong, and help him feel better. When Megan was having a bad day, she'd still ask Alex how his day went and listen to his problems while managing her own emotions privately.

When they had relationship issues, Megan would bring them up, guide the conversation, and take responsibility for finding solutions. Alex would participate when prompted but rarely started discussions about their relationship health.

When they socialized with friends or family, Megan would coordinate plans, manage social dynamics, and make sure everyone felt included. Alex would show up and enjoy the events without thinking about the work required to make them happen.

In my marriage it was completely one-sided, except the roles were reversed. I cooked, cleaned, worked to finance everything, kept Claudia entertained, and nursed her through eight years of chronic illness. She contributed when there was something in it for her. Otherwise it simply didn't happen. I didn't understand at the time that this wasn't just a personality difference — it was who she was. Some people are incapable of giving without a transaction attached. You can't fix that with better communication.

This pattern meant Megan was doing most of the emotional work while Alex was benefiting from her efforts without contributing equally.

Some people take responsibility for maintaining contact, remembering important events, and managing the emotional health of friendships. Other people participate when prompted but don't take initiative for relationship maintenance.

High emotional labor people feel like they're doing all the work to maintain relationships. Low emotional labor people feel like their friends or partners are being controlling or demanding when asked to contribute more.

Megan eventually told Alex that she couldn't continue being solely responsible for their emotional connection. She needed him to take the initiative in noticing her moods, bringing up relationship issues, and contributing to their social coordination.

Alex initially reacted defensively. He pointed out all the practical things he did for their relationship and said he didn't understand why Megan was making simple things complicated. He accused her of trying to change his personality.

But Megan wasn't asking Alex to become a different person. She was asking him to take equal responsibility for the emotional work that relationships require.

Alex learned to pay attention to Megan's emotional state without being prompted. He started conversations about their relationship instead of waiting for Megan to bring up issues.

Megan stopped automatically managing everything and let Alex carry his share.

Neither of them became a different person. They just stopped assuming the other one wasn't capable.

Chapter 14: Risk Tolerance Differences

How much uncertainty can you actually live with?

Not theoretically. Not in the abstract. Really — if the income stopped tomorrow, if the plan changed, if the sure thing turned out not to be sure — how long before you panic, and what does that panic make you do?

Most people have never thought hard about this. They find out their answer when something forces the question, usually when they're in a relationship with someone whose answer is completely different from theirs.

Risk tolerance is one of those things that's invisible until it isn't. Two people can date for years and never discover they have opposite relationships with uncertainty because nothing has pushed hard enough to reveal it. Then one person wants to quit their job, start a business, move across the country, or make a financial bet on something unproven — and suddenly they're not just disagreeing about a decision. They're running on completely different operating systems.

This is the risk tolerance divide, and it creates conflict in relationships when people assume their partner should share their comfort level with uncertainty.

Ben had a high risk tolerance. He was comfortable with uncertainty, excited by new challenges, and willing to sacrifice security for opportunity. He'd rather try and fail than wonder what could have been. For him, the biggest risk was staying stuck in a situation that didn't fulfill him.

Sarah had a low risk tolerance. She was uncomfortable with uncertainty, stressed by unpredictable situations, and willing to sacrifice opportunity for security. She'd rather have steady but boring than exciting but unstable. For her, the biggest risk was losing the stability they'd already built.

Neither approach was wrong, but they were incompatible when both people expected their partner to share their risk assessment.

Ben couldn't understand why Sarah didn't share his excitement about the business opportunity. He thought if she really believed in him, she'd support his entrepreneurial ambitions instead of focusing on worst-case scenarios. Her concerns felt like a lack of faith in his abilities.

Sarah couldn't understand why Ben was willing to gamble their financial security on an unproven idea. She thought that if he really cared about their future together, he'd prioritize stability over his personal ambitions. His plans felt like he was putting his desires ahead of their relationship.

Both interpretations missed the fact that they were operating from different relationships with risk and uncertainty.

High-risk tolerance people want to try new things, move to different places, make big changes, and take chances. Low risk tolerance people want to research extensively, plan carefully, save money, and avoid unnecessary uncertainty.

High-risk tolerance people see their partners' caution as fear and limitation. Low risk tolerance people see their partners' adventurousness as recklessness and selfishness.

Neither perspective is accurate because they're based on different comfort levels with unknown outcomes.

Ben's willingness to start a business wasn't about being irresponsible or not caring about their future. It was about his natural comfort with uncertainty and his belief that calculated risks lead to better outcomes.

Sarah's preference for stability wasn't about being fearful or not believing in Ben. It was about her natural need for security and her belief that steady progress leads to better outcomes.

The problem came when they tried to convince the other person their risk assessment was objectively correct.

Ben tried to show Sarah data about successful entrepreneurs and statistics about business growth. Sarah tried to show Ben data about business failure rates and the importance of emergency savings.

Both approaches missed the point because they weren't really arguing about data. They were arguing about comfort levels with uncertainty.

Ben learned that Sarah's need for security wasn't about a lack of ambition or faith in him. It was about how her brain processed uncertainty and potential loss. He could pursue his business goals while also addressing her legitimate security concerns.

Sarah learned that Ben's willingness to take risks wasn't about being careless or selfish. It was about how his brain processed opportunity and potential gain. She could support his ambitions while also maintaining the security measures that made her comfortable.

They found a compromise where Ben started his business while maintaining enough financial cushion to address Sarah's security needs. Ben got to pursue his opportunity, and Sarah got to maintain her peace of mind.

This required them to stop judging the other person's risk tolerance and start working with it.

High-risk tolerance people want to be spontaneous and try new shit. Low risk tolerance people want to plan and stick with known quantities.

Risk tolerance differences don't mean one person always gets their way. It means finding approaches that acknowledge both people's comfort levels with uncertainty instead of assuming everyone should share the same relationship with risk.

Chapter 15: Documentation and Self-Protection

When Kyle's ex-girlfriend Rachel started telling their mutual friends that he'd been abusive during their relationship, Kyle had no way to defend himself. He hadn't saved any of their text conversations. He couldn't prove that Rachel had been the one who started most of their fights or that she'd threatened to hurt herself when he tried to leave. All he had was his word against hers, and she was a better storyteller.

Rachel wasn't lying about everything, but she was twisting the truth to make herself look like a victim and Kyle appear to be an abuser. She conveniently forgot about the times she'd thrown things at him, the times she'd screamed at him in public, or the times she'd manipulated him with suicide threats. Her version of their relationship bore little resemblance to what happened.

Documentation matters in relationships, especially when dealing with manipulative or unstable people.

Kyle thought keeping records of relationship conflicts was paranoid and unromantic. He believed that if you loved someone, trust them and assume good intentions. He deleted angry text exchanges after they made up and never wrote down specific incidents when Rachel acted out.

This mindset left him completely fucked when Rachel rewrote their relationship history to benefit her narrative.

Rachel had a pattern of creating drama, escalating conflicts, and then playing victim when consequences arrived. She'd start fights, push Kyle until he reacted, and then focus on his reaction while ignoring her own behavior. When their relationship ended, she used the same pattern to destroy his reputation.

Kyle learned too late that some people will lie about you to protect themselves, gain sympathy, or get revenge. Without documentation, you have no defense against false accusations.

Documentation doesn't mean you're planning to sue someone or expecting the worst. It means you're protecting yourself against people who might rewrite history to suit their needs.

Save text messages, especially ones that show patterns of manipulation, threats, or abusive behavior. Screenshot social media posts before they get deleted. Keep records of important conversations, including dates and witnesses when possible.

This isn't about being paranoid or distrustful. It's about recognizing that some people will throw you under the bus to save themselves, and you need evidence to defend against false narratives.

Kyle's friends initially believed Rachel's version of events because she told an engaging story about being trapped in an abusive relationship. Kyle's protests that Rachel was lying sounded defensive and self-serving. Without evidence to back up his claims, he looked like an abuser trying to avoid responsibility.

Rachel knew exactly what she was doing. She'd learned that playing the victim was more effective than taking responsibility for her own behavior. She could manipulate people's emotions and gain sympathy while destroying Kyle's reputation.

Kyle eventually found some old emails that showed Rachel threatening suicide when he tried to break up with her. He also found witnesses who'd seen Rachel attack him physically during one of their public fights. This evidence helped some people understand that Rachel's story wasn't the whole truth.

But the damage was already done. Kyle lost several friendships and had to deal with his reputation being destroyed in their social circle.

Documentation becomes especially important when dealing with people who have personality disorders, addiction problems, or histories of manipulation. These people often use relationships as weapons and will destroy you to protect themselves.

Always document threats, both explicit and implied. Document instances of physical violence, including throwing objects or blocking exits. Document manipulation tactics like threatening self-harm to control behavior. Document lies, both small and large, that show patterns of dishonesty.

This information protects you legally if the person escalates false accusations of abuse, harassment, or stalking. It also protects you socially when the person tries to turn mutual friends against you.

Kyle wishes he'd understood that Rachel's dramatic stories about her ex-boyfriends should have been a warning sign. She claimed every ex was abusive, crazy, or stalked her. Kyle thought he was different, and that Rachel had just been unlucky in love.

He didn't realize that when someone claims every ex was the problem, they're usually the problem themselves.

Documentation also helps you recognize your own patterns and behavior. When you write out what happened during conflicts, you can see whether you're being manipulated or if you're contributing to dysfunction.

Kyle realized through documentation that Rachel would create crises whenever he tried to establish boundaries or spend time away from her. She'd manufacture emergencies, start fights, or threaten self-harm to regain his attention and control.

Seeing this pattern on paper helped Kyle understand he wasn't going crazy and that Rachel's behavior was genuinely manipulative.

Documentation doesn't make you a bad person or mean you don't trust your partner. It makes you someone who protects themselves against people who might use your vulnerability against you.

Start documenting any relationship that involves frequent drama, emotional manipulation, threats, or patterns of dishonesty. Your future self will thank you when you need evidence to defend against false accusations or gaslighting.

Chapter 16: Building Pattern-Proof Relationship Skills

After going through seventeen chapters of relationship problems, you might wonder how the hell you're supposed to navigate all these patterns without losing your mind. The answer isn't to memorize every communication style and personality difference. The answer is to develop skills that work regardless of what patterns you encounter.

Pattern-proof relationship skills are communication and boundary techniques that function across different personality types, gender differences, and relationship dynamics. Instead of trying to diagnose every person you meet, you learn to respond effectively to whatever they throw at you.

The first pattern-proof skill is direct communication. Instead of trying to figure out whether someone is a hinter or a direct communicator, you communicate clearly and ask for clarification when you're confused.

When someone says something vague like, "I'm fine," instead of guessing whether they mean it or trying to decode their hidden message, you say, "I'm getting mixed signals. Can you tell me directly what you need right now?"

When someone seems upset but won't tell you why, instead of playing detective or assuming you did something wrong, you say, "I can see you're upset. Do you want to talk about it, or do you need space to process?"

Direct communication cuts through most of the bullshit patterns that create relationship problems. You stop trying to read minds and start asking people to be clear about what they want.

The second pattern-proof skill is boundary setting. Instead of trying to accommodate every person's needs and preferences, you establish clear limits about what you will and won't do in relationships.

When someone expects you to manage their emotions, you say, "I care about you, but I can't be responsible for fixing your mood. What can you do to take care of yourself right now?"

When someone pressures you to violate your own needs, you say, "I understand this is important to you, but I'm not available for that. Here's what I can do instead."

Boundary setting works regardless of whether someone is high-maintenance, manipulative, or just has different needs than you do. You protect your own wellbeing while still treating them with respect.

The third pattern-proof skill is emotional regulation. Instead of taking other people's moods and behaviors personally, you maintain your own emotional equilibrium regardless of what's happening around you.

When someone is having a bad day and taking it out on you, you recognize it's about their emotional state, not your actions. You don't absorb their stress or feel responsible for fixing their problems.

When someone rejects your ideas or doesn't respond the way you expected, you don't immediately assume you did something wrong or that they don't care about you. You consider alternative explanations before making it about yourself.

Emotional regulation prevents you from getting sucked into other people's drama and dysfunction. You can respond thoughtfully instead of reacting emotionally to every situation.

The fourth pattern-proof skill is reality testing. Instead of accepting other people's version of events at face value, you verify information and trust your own observations.

When someone tells you a story that doesn't match your experience, you say, "That's not how I remember it. Let me tell you what I observed."

When someone tries to convince you that your feelings or perceptions are wrong, you trust your own experience while remaining open to their perspective.

Reality testing protects you from gaslighting and manipulation. You maintain your own sense of what's true instead of letting other people rewrite reality for you.

The fifth pattern-proof skill is flexible problem-solving. Instead of insisting on one approach to every situation, you adapt your response based on what's happening.

When direct communication isn't working, you try a different approach. When boundaries aren't being respected, you escalate consequences. When someone needs space, you give it. When someone needs connection, you provide it.

Flexible problem-solving means you're not locked into rigid strategies that only work with certain personality types. You can adjust your approach based on what's effective in each specific situation.

These five skills work together to create relationships that function well regardless of the personalities involved. You don't need to become an expert in every relationship pattern. You just need to communicate clearly, set boundaries, regulate your emotions, test reality, and solve problems flexibly.

The goal isn't to find perfect people who never trigger any of these patterns. The goal is to develop the skills to handle whatever patterns show up without losing yourself in the process.

Pattern-proof skills also help you identify which relationships are worth investing in and which ones are too fucked up to maintain. When you're communicating clearly and setting boundaries, healthy people will work with you. Unhealthy people will fight you every step of the way.

People who respond well to direct communication, respect your boundaries, don't manipulate your emotions, accept reality, and work with you to solve problems are relationship material. People who fight these basic relationship skills are not.

Part 2: The Bullshit That Happens When Someone Is Broken

Everything in Part 1 assumed you were dealing with a normal person.

Someone who processes stress differently than you. Someone who needs more space or more connection. Someone who shows love through actions instead of words, or communicates through hints instead of asking directly. Frustrating, sometimes. Confusing, often. But fundamentally decent, and workable if both people are willing to figure it out.

Part 2 is different.

The people in these chapters aren't just wired differently. They're using you. They're lying to you. They're systematically dismantling your ability to trust your own perceptions. They're manipulating your protective instincts against you, or isolating you from everyone who might help you see what's happening.

You can't communicate your way out of this. You can't compromise with it. Understanding why they do what they do doesn't make it manageable — it just tells you what you're actually dealing with.

The patterns here aren't relationship problems. They're predatory behavior, personality disorders, and psychological abuse dressed up as relationship problems. The difference matters because the response is completely different. Normal relationship problems call for patience, understanding, and better communication. The shit in Part 2 calls for documentation, boundaries, and usually an exit.

Learn to tell the difference. It might save you a decade.

Chapter 17: Toxic Femininity Patterns

When Josh's girlfriend Lauren was upset about something, she wouldn't tell him what was wrong. Instead, she'd become cold and distant, give him one-word answers, and act like everything was fine when he asked directly. When Josh finally got frustrated and raised his voice, Lauren would immediately start crying and accuse him of being aggressive and scary.

This happened every few weeks. Lauren would get upset about something, refuse to communicate about it directly, create tension until Josh reacted emotionally, and then use his reaction as evidence that he was the problem. Josh would end up apologizing for getting frustrated while the original issue never got addressed.

Lauren was using toxic femininity patterns to manipulate Josh and avoid accountability for her own behavior.

Toxic femininity is the flip side of toxic masculinity. It's when women use traditionally feminine traits like emotional sensitivity, victimhood, and social manipulation as weapons to control others and avoid taking responsibility for their actions.

Just like toxic masculinity doesn't represent all men, toxic femininity doesn't represent all women. But these patterns are common enough that men need to recognize them and know how to respond.

Lauren wasn't unique. The specific tactics women use to manipulate and avoid accountability follow recognizable patterns once you know what you're looking for.

The most common is weaponizing emotions — turning tears, breakdowns, or claims of being triggered into a conversation-stopper. The moment you try to hold them accountable, the emotional volume goes up and suddenly you're the problem for upsetting them. Their reaction becomes your responsibility, and the original issue disappears.

Closely related is playing the victim. Whatever they did wrong, whatever they started, by the end of the conversation they've repositioned themselves as the injured party and you as the aggressor. It doesn't matter what happened. They're better at controlling the narrative than you are.

Then there's passive-aggressive communication — refusing to say what's wrong, going cold, giving one-word answers, and then punishing you for not reading their mind. They manufacture tension without ever taking ownership of it. When you finally react, that reaction becomes proof that you're the real problem.

Social manipulation is the long game version. Threats to tell friends or family you're abusive. Gossip designed to damage your reputation before you can tell your side. Turning your mutual social circle against you preemptively so that if you ever leave or push back, you're already the villain.

Sexual manipulation is using intimacy as a control mechanism — withholding it when you don't comply, offering it when you do. Sex stops being about connection and becomes a behavioral lever.

Emotional blackmail is the most dangerous. Threatening self-harm or suicide to prevent you from leaving or setting a boundary. They've figured out that your concern for their wellbeing can be used against you, and they use it without hesitation.

And false fragility — playing helpless to avoid responsibility or to get others to do things for them. They're not incapable. They've just learned that performing vulnerability gets results.

Lauren used several of these patterns with Josh. She'd weaponize her emotions by crying whenever he tried to address her behavior. She'd play victim by making his frustration the problem instead of her refusal to communicate. She used passive-aggressive communication to create conflict without taking responsibility for starting it.

Toxic femininity exploits men's protective instincts and social conditioning. Men are taught to be gentle with women, to prioritize women's emotional needs, and to take responsibility for women's feelings. Toxic women exploit this conditioning to avoid accountability.

Josh felt like he couldn't push back against Lauren's behavior because she was "sensitive" and he didn't want to hurt her feelings. He ended up walking on eggshells, managing her emotions, and accepting blame for problems he didn't create.

Protecting yourself starts with refusing to accept responsibility for someone else's emotional reactions. When they try to make their feelings your fault, redirect back to whatever was actually being discussed. Don't let the conversation get hijacked by their response to the conversation.

When someone uses tears or a breakdown to shut things down, name it directly. Not cruelly, but clearly. You're not required to pause every difficult conversation because the other person finds it uncomfortable. If they're not ready to engage, they can say so — but the issue doesn't go away.

Emotional blackmail requires a specific response: take the threat seriously by involving the appropriate people — a crisis line, emergency services if needed — but don't change your behavior to manage it. The moment you comply with a demand backed by a self-harm threat, you've confirmed that it works. It will be used again.

Passive-aggressive behavior deserves a simple response: you're not going to guess. When they're ready to say directly what's wrong, you're ready to listen. Until then, you're done trying to decode the silence.

Document everything that feels like a pattern. Threats, incidents, manipulative exchanges. Not because you're planning to use it immediately, but because these people are skilled at rewriting history and you'll need your own record of what happened.

Most importantly — stop rewarding the behavior with engagement. When manipulation gets attention, compliance, or an apology it didn't earn, it gets repeated. Remove yourself from the situation. Don't lecture, don't argue, don't try to make them see what they're doing. Just stop participating.

The hardest part about dealing with toxic femininity is that society often supports these behaviors. Women who use emotional manipulation are seen as "sensitive" instead of manipulative. Men who push back against these patterns are labeled as "aggressive" or "unsympathetic."

Josh eventually realized that Lauren's emotional reactions weren't about sensitivity. They were about control. She used tears and claims of being hurt to shut down any conversation that might hold her accountable for her behavior.

Once Josh understood this, he stopped accepting responsibility for Lauren's emotions and started insisting on direct communication. Lauren escalated her manipulation tactics, but Josh held firm. Eventually, Lauren found someone else who was willing to manage her emotions for her.

Toxic femininity patterns work because they exploit men's desire to be good partners and protectors. But protecting someone shouldn't mean accepting manipulation and abuse. Women can take responsibility for their own emotions and behavior, and expecting them to do so isn't cruel or insensitive.

Some of these behaviors develop from real pain and real history. That doesn't make them acceptable and it doesn't make them your problem to fix.

If you're in a relationship with someone who consistently uses these patterns, you're not dealing with sensitivity or vulnerability. You're dealing with manipulation and emotional abuse. Protect yourself accordingly.

Chapter 18: Male Manipulation Tactics

When Sarah first met Marcus, he was the perfect boyfriend. He showered her with attention, expensive gifts, and constant declarations of love. He told her she was different from every other woman he'd met and that he'd never felt this way about anyone before. Within three weeks, he was talking about moving in together and planning their future.

Six months later, Marcus had isolated Sarah from her friends, convinced her to quit her job to spend more time with him, and was controlling every aspect of her daily life. When Sarah tried to reconnect with old friends, Marcus had a crisis that required her immediate attention. When she mentioned wanting to go back to work, Marcus would remind her how much he was providing for her and question why she didn't appreciate his generosity.

Sarah had been love-bombed, isolated, and financially controlled by a master manipulator who used traditionally masculine traits like providing and protecting as weapons.

Male manipulation tends to use different tools than female manipulation, but the goal is the same: control through dependence.

Love bombing is usually the opening move. Overwhelming attention, constant contact, declarations of love within weeks, talk of the future before you've had time to see who this person actually is. It feels like intensity and chemistry. It's actually about hooking you emotionally before your judgment catches up. Healthy attraction develops. It doesn't arrive fully formed in week two.

Financial control is how physical dependence gets built. Encouraging or pressuring a partner to leave her job. Controlling access to money. Running up debt in her name. Making her feel grateful for being provided for while quietly removing every option she'd need to leave. Marcus didn't look like a controller — he looked like a provider. That's the point.

Isolation is the slow one. It doesn't happen in a dramatic moment. It happens through a hundred small crises, each one pulling her attention back to him whenever she tries to invest in anyone else. Friends become sources of drama. Family becomes intrusive. Eventually he's the only relationship she has left, which means he's the only one she can turn to when things get bad.

Intimidation doesn't require violence. Size, anger, a certain look, the way someone moves when they're displeased — these things communicate threat without a single word. A man who has never hit anyone can still make a woman feel physically unsafe, and that fear shapes her behavior just as effectively as if he had.

Sexual coercion is pressure, guilt, and manipulation applied to physical intimacy. Using her love for him against her. Framing her reluctance as a relationship problem. Wearing her down until compliance feels easier than another argument.

Gaslighting is denying reality until she stops trusting her own perception of it. He didn't say that. She's remembering it wrong. She's too sensitive. She's crazy. Applied consistently over time, it works. People start to doubt themselves when the person closest to them insists their experience isn't real.

Marcus used several of these tactics with Sarah. The love-bombing phase made Sarah feel like she'd found her soulmate. The financial control made her dependent on him for basic security. The isolation tactics cut her off from people who might have helped her see what was happening.

Male manipulation often masquerades as traditional masculine virtues. Marcus presented his financial control as being a good provider. His isolation tactics looked like wanting to spend time with her. His possessiveness seemed like protection and devotion.

Sarah thought she was lucky to have found a man who was so committed to her and their relationship. She didn't realize that his "devotion" was about ownership and control.

The first thing to understand is that love bombing is a tactic, not a feeling. When someone is moving fast — too much too soon, future talk before you know each other, intensity that feels almost overwhelming — that's not passion. That's pressure. Slow it down deliberately and watch how they respond. Someone who's genuinely into you will respect the pace. Someone who's running a play will get frustrated or escalate.

Financial independence isn't negotiable. Don't quit your job for someone you're dating. Don't hand over access to your accounts. Don't let someone else become your only source of income or security. Having your own money isn't a sign that you don't trust him. It's the thing that gives you an actual choice if you ever need one.

Your social connections are not optional. If spending time with friends or family consistently generates conflict, crisis, or guilt from your partner, that's not a relationship problem — that's isolation in progress. Real partners don't compete with your other relationships. They understand that a person with a full life is healthier and happier to be with.

Trust your body's response to someone's anger. If his displeasure makes you feel physically careful — if you find yourself monitoring his mood, adjusting your behavior to avoid triggering him, feeling a kind of low-level fear you can't quite name — that's information. That's not normal relationship tension.

Document what happens. Controlling behavior, threats, incidents you find yourself second-guessing later. Manipulators are good at making their targets doubt their own memory, and a written record from the time it happened is hard to argue with.

The clearest signal that something is wrong is feeling like you're disappearing. If you've stopped seeing people you used to see, stopped doing things you used to do, stopped knowing what you actually think and want — pay attention to that. It didn't happen all at once. But it happened for a reason.

The hardest part about escaping male manipulation is that it often feels like love and protection. Marcus genuinely seemed to care about Sarah's wellbeing and safety. He just wanted those things to depend completely on him.

Sarah eventually realized that Marcus's "love" came with too many conditions and restrictions. Real love doesn't require you to give up your autonomy, friends, or financial independence. Real protection doesn't involve isolating you from other sources of support.

Male manipulators often target women who are going through transitions or vulnerabilities. They look for women who are new to an area, dealing with family problems, or struggling financially. They present themselves as solutions to these problems while making them worse.

Marcus targeted Sarah when she was new to the city and didn't have established social connections. He positioned himself as her guide and protector in an unfamiliar place, then used that role to prevent her from developing independence.

None of this means assuming all men are manipulative. Most men are capable of healthy relationships that don't involve control and dominance. But recognizing these patterns helps you identify the ones who aren't.

If you're in a relationship where you feel like you're losing yourself, walking on eggshells, or becoming increasingly dependent on your partner, you might be dealing with manipulation instead of love. Trust your instincts and reach out for support before you lose more of your autonomy and independence.

Chapter 19: The Crap Fathers Teach Their Sons

When Brad's dad caught him crying after his girlfriend broke up with him in high school, his father's response was immediate and brutal: "Stop acting like a little bitch. Real men don't cry over women. There are plenty of fish in the sea."

Brad learned two things that day: emotions make you weak, and women are replaceable objects instead of human beings. These lessons fucked up every relationship he had for the next twenty years.

This is how toxic masculinity gets passed down from generation to generation. Fathers who never learned healthy relationship skills teach their sons the same dysfunctional bullshit that destroyed their own marriages and friendships. The cycle continues because nobody wants to admit that Dad was wrong about women, emotions, and what it means to be a man.

Most of it gets passed down without anyone questioning whether it works. Dad didn't mean to sabotage his son's relationships. He was just repeating what he'd been told.

"Real men don't show emotions" creates men who can't connect with women, can't process their own feelings, and think vulnerability is weakness. Women can't form deep connections with men who are emotionally unavailable, so these men end up in shallow relationships or alone.

"Women are impossible to understand" teaches sons that women are a different species instead of individual human beings. It excuses men from learning basic communication skills and creates an us-versus-them mentality that makes friendship impossible.

"Don't let women walk all over you" turns every disagreement into a power struggle. Sons learn to see women's needs as attempts to control them instead of learning how to compromise and work together as partners.

"You have to be the provider and protector" creates men who think their only value is financial and physical. It ignores that women want partners, not servants, and sets up relationships where men feel used and women feel like children.

"Women only want your money" creates cynical men who can't trust women's interest. They either attract gold diggers because that's what they expect, or they sabotage healthy relationships by constantly questioning women's motives.

"Boys will be boys" excuses bad behavior instead of teaching accountability. Sons learn that being male means they can't control themselves and that women should accept their flaws instead of expecting them to grow.

"Never trust a woman completely" creates men who are constantly looking for evidence of betrayal instead of building secure relationships. When you treat someone like they're going to betray you, they often do.

Brad's father taught him most of these lessons through example and direct instruction. Brad learned that showing weakness meant losing respect, that women were manipulative creatures who needed to be managed, and that real men solved problems through dominance instead of communication.

These lessons served Brad poorly in relationships. He attracted women who were impressed by his emotional distance and financial success, but he couldn't maintain long-term connections because he never learned how to be vulnerable, honest, or genuinely supportive.

When women tried to connect with him emotionally, Brad saw it as neediness. When they expressed their own needs, he saw it as attempts to control him. When they got frustrated with his lack of emotional availability, he saw it as proof that women were impossible to please.

The real tragedy is that Brad's father was teaching him lessons that didn't even work for his own generation. Brad's parents divorced when he was sixteen, partly because his father couldn't emotionally connect with his mother and treated every marital disagreement as a battle he had to win.

But Brad's father couldn't admit his approach was wrong, so he doubled down on the same advice that had destroyed his own marriage.

Here's what to teach instead.

Emotions are information, not weakness. Men who can process feelings are better partners, better friends, and more successful. Teach your sons that vulnerability creates connection, not loss of respect.

Women are individuals, not a category. Each woman has her own personality, needs, and communication style. Learning to see women as people instead of puzzles to solve is the foundation of healthy relationships.

Compromise isn't losing. Healthy relationships require both people to give and take. Teaching your son that meeting someone halfway makes him weak sets him up for relationships where nobody's needs get met.

Your value isn't just what you provide financially. Women want partners who are interesting, supportive, and present. Money is a nice bonus, not the foundation of lasting attraction.

Trust is earned and given. Teach your sons how to recognize trustworthy behavior instead of assuming all women are out to get them. Also teach them how to be trustworthy themselves.

Take responsibility for your actions. Being a man means being accountable for your behavior, learning from your mistakes, and growing. It doesn't mean making excuses or blaming others when things go wrong.

Brad eventually learned these lessons, but it took him until his thirties and the end of two serious relationships. He had to unlearn everything his father taught him about masculinity and relationships.

The process was painful because it meant admitting that his father was wrong about fundamental aspects of life. It also meant recognizing that his relationship failures weren't women's fault; they were the result of toxic beliefs he'd inherited and never questioned.

Fathers have enormous influence over how their sons approach relationships. The lessons you teach your son about emotions, communication, and women will shape every romantic relationship he has for the rest of his life.

If you're a father, ask yourself: Are you teaching your son skills that will help him build healthy relationships, or are you passing down the same dysfunction that previous generations handed to you?

If you're a son dealing with toxic lessons from your father, understand that unlearning this stuff is possible but requires conscious effort. You're not doomed to repeat your father's mistakes, but you have to actively choose to do things differently.

The goal isn't to blame fathers for relationship problems. The goal is to recognize that much of what gets passed down as masculine wisdom is outdated bullshit that creates more problems than it solves.

Break the cycle. Teach the next generation of men how to build relationships based on mutual respect, honest communication, and genuine connection instead of dominance, emotional suppression, and mistrust.

Your sons deserve better relationship skills than you probably received. Give them the tools to build the kinds of connections that work.

Chapter 20: The Stupid Shit Mothers Teach Their Sons

When Kevin's girlfriend Sarah broke up with him after six months of dating, his mother's response was immediate and predictable: "She doesn't know what she's losing, honey. You're such a good man. Any woman would be lucky to have you. She'll realize her mistake and come back."

Kevin spent the next three years waiting for Sarah to "come to her senses" and return to him. He turned down other dating opportunities because his mother had convinced him that being a "good man" meant Sarah owed him love and would eventually recognize his worth.

Sarah never came back. She was happily dating someone else within two months and married him within two years. Kevin remained single, bitter, and confused about why being "good" wasn't enough to keep a woman.

This is how mothers create nice guys who can't understand why women don't want them.

Most mothers have no idea they're sabotaging their sons' romantic futures. They think they're building confidence and teaching respect for women. In reality, they're creating entitled, passive men who expect relationships to work like their relationship with their mother: unconditional love in exchange for being "good."

The damage is usually well-intentioned. Mothers who love their sons want to protect them from rejection and heartbreak. What they actually create are men who can't form healthy relationships because they've been taught fundamentally wrong things about what women want.

"You need to find a nice girl to take care of you" teaches sons that women exist to serve them. It creates men who look for maternal figures instead of partners and expect women to manage their emotions, cook their meals, and handle their problems.

"Women are more emotional and sensitive than men" reinforces stereotypes that make it impossible to understand women as individuals. Sons learn to treat all women like fragile creatures who need protecting from reality instead of capable adults who can handle honesty and conflict.

"Always put women on a pedestal" creates men who worship women instead of treating them as equals. Pedestal treatment feels suffocating because it's based on an idealized fantasy, not on who the person actually is.

"If you're good to her, she'll love you forever" teaches a transactional view where kindness equals romantic obligation. Sons learn that being nice should automatically result in love, sex, and commitment, regardless of compatibility or attraction.

"Women don't enjoy sex like men do" creates sexual shame and misunderstanding that destroys intimacy. Sons learn to see female sexuality as something they have to convince women to participate in, instead of understanding that women want good sex with men they're attracted to.

"You should never make a woman upset" teaches conflict avoidance instead of healthy communication. Sons learn to suppress their own needs and opinions to avoid any disagreement, creating relationships where problems never get resolved and resentment builds quietly.

"Find someone who needs you" attracts codependent dynamics where the man's worth depends on solving a woman's problems. Both people end up damaged and using each other instead of building something healthy.

"Real love means never having to ask for what you want" teaches the mind-reading expectation that destroys relationships. Sons learn that if a woman really loves them, she'll automatically know what they need without being told.

Kevin's mother taught him several of these lessons. She constantly praised him for being "such a good boy" and told him that someday he'd find "a girl who appreciates you." She also complained about his father's emotional unavailability, teaching Kevin that women wanted men who were sensitive and emotionally accessible.

Kevin learned that his value came from being good, nice, and emotionally available. He learned that women were delicate creatures who needed protection and care. He learned that if he was patient and kind enough, any woman would eventually fall in love with him.

These lessons turned Kevin into a classic nice guy. He was attracted to women who seemed to need rescuing. He put women on pedestals and treated them like precious objects instead of real people. He avoided any conflict or disagreement because he thought that would make women uncomfortable.

When women didn't respond to his niceness with immediate attraction and gratitude, Kevin felt confused and resentful. He'd done everything his mother taught him was right. Why weren't women appreciating his efforts?

The problem was that Kevin's mother had taught him to be a good son, not a good partner. The qualities that make mothers love their sons unconditionally are not the same qualities that create romantic attraction and sustainable relationships.

Women don't want sons. They want partners. They want men who can challenge them, disagree with them, and treat them as equals instead of fragile creatures who need constant care and protection.

Kevin's approach backfired because it was based on fundamental misunderstandings about female psychology. Women aren't attracted to men who worship them. They're attracted to men who see them as complete human beings worth knowing, not problems worth solving.

The nice guy approach also creates entitled thinking. When you believe that being good should automatically result in love, you start to resent women who don't reciprocate your feelings. Kevin eventually became bitter toward women who rejected him, even though they'd never asked for his niceness and didn't owe him anything in return.

Here's what to teach instead.

Women want partners, not servants. Healthy relationships are between equals who support each other, not one person taking care of the other like a parent.

Attraction isn't a choice and it can't be earned through good behavior. Women can appreciate kind, respectful men without being romantically interested in them. Those are different things.

Conflict is normal and healthy. Disagreements are part of relationships. Avoiding conflict doesn't make a relationship stronger — it makes it shallow and unsustainable.

A man's worth isn't determined by female approval. Self-esteem built through personal accomplishment and character lasts. Self-esteem built through romantic validation collapses the moment she stops validating.

Rejection isn't personal failure. Not every woman will be interested, and that doesn't mean anything is wrong with him or her. Teach your sons to handle rejection without taking it as a verdict on their worth.

Be authentic instead of just nice. Express genuine thoughts and feelings instead of always trying to be agreeable and accommodating. Niceness without authenticity is just performance, and people see through it.

Kevin eventually learned these lessons, but it took him until his late twenties and several painful rejections. He had to unlearn his mother's well-intentioned but misguided advice about what women wanted.

The process was difficult because it meant accepting that his mother was wrong about relationships and that his entire approach to dating had been counterproductive. It also meant developing the kind of confidence and authenticity that his mother's overprotection had prevented him from building.

Mothers who overprotect their sons from emotional pain end up making them less capable of handling the normal ups and downs of adult relationships. Sons who are shielded from rejection, conflict, and disappointment don't develop the resilience needed for healthy romantic connections.

The most damaging lesson mothers teach is that love should be unconditional and automatic. Maternal love works this way, but romantic love doesn't. Romantic relationships require ongoing effort, compatibility, attraction, and choice from both people.

When mothers teach sons to expect romantic love to work like maternal love, they set them up for constant disappointment and resentment. Adult relationships require negotiation, compromise, and the ability to handle the fact that sometimes love isn't enough.

If you're a mother, examine the messages you're sending your son about relationships. Are you teaching him skills that will help him build healthy partnerships, or are you preparing him to be a good son who expects women to love him the way you do?

If you're a son dealing with nice guy programming from your mother, understand that unlearning this mindset is essential for relationship success. You're not entitled to love because you're good. You're not responsible for protecting women from reality. And you don't need female approval to be valuable.

Develop your own identity, interests, and confidence. Learn to handle rejection without taking it personally. Practice being authentic instead of just being nice. These skills will serve you better than all the well-meaning but misguided advice your mother gave you about being a good boy.

Women want men, not boys. Stop trying to be the perfect son and start learning to be an authentic partner.

Chapter 21: Society's Bullshit

When Mark was growing up, every movie he watched taught him the same lesson: if you love someone enough, everything will work out. It didn't matter if she was dating someone else, lived across the country, or had completely different life goals. Love conquered all. Grand gestures fixed everything. And if it was "meant to be," the universe would make it happen.

Mark spent his twenties chasing women who weren't interested, making grand romantic gestures that came across as creepy, and waiting for the universe to deliver his soulmate. He went through a series of failed relationships because he'd been programmed by society to believe in fairy tale bullshit that has nothing to do with how real relationships work.

Society feeds us toxic relationship advice from birth through death. Movies, TV shows, social media, songs, books, and cultural messaging all promote ideas about love and relationships that are not just wrong—they're actively destructive. Most people absorb these messages without questioning them and wonder why their relationships keep failing.

The relationship advice industry makes billions selling hope and fantasy instead of practical skills. Social media creates fake relationship standards that real couples can't meet. Entertainment teaches us that dysfunction and drama equal passion and love.

The myths start early and go deep.

"Love conquers all" is probably the most damaging. Love doesn't conquer fundamental incompatibility, addiction, financial irresponsibility, or abusive behavior. It's necessary but not sufficient. You also need respect, compatibility, shared values, and basic emotional health.

"You'll know when you meet the one" creates unrealistic expectations about how attraction and compatibility work. Most successful relationships develop gradually through getting to know someone, not through instant cosmic recognition. The soulmate myth makes people reject perfectly good partners because the feeling isn't magical from day one.

"If you have to work at it, it's not meant to be" teaches people to quit the moment a relationship requires effort. All healthy relationships require work, communication, and compromise. Believing otherwise sets people up to abandon things worth keeping.

"Just be yourself" is terrible advice for people whose natural selves are socially awkward, selfish, or emotionally immature. Sometimes you need to grow. Being yourself only works if yourself is someone worth being around.

"Opposites attract" confuses chemistry with compatibility. While some differences complement each other, fundamental opposites create constant conflict. Different values, life goals, and approaches to money, sex, and family cause ongoing problems that passion can't fix.

"Grand gestures fix everything" is movie nonsense. Grand gestures are often manipulation tactics that avoid addressing real issues. What women want is consistent daily respect and consideration, not expensive performances that substitute for genuine effort.

"There's someone for everyone" prevents people from doing the work necessary to become relationship material. Some people are too damaged or selfish for healthy relationships until they address their issues. Telling them to keep looking instead of fixing themselves wastes everyone's time.

"Happy wife, happy life" teaches men that their own needs don't matter. It creates relationships where men become resentful servants and women lose respect for partners who won't stand up for themselves.

"You complete me" teaches people to look for partners to fill their emotional holes instead of becoming whole themselves. It creates relationships where both people lose their individual identities and depend on each other for basic stability.

"Love yourself first" is used as an excuse to never enter relationships at all. Some people discover who they are through the process of dating and relating to others. Waiting until you're complete means waiting forever.

Mark absorbed all of these messages and structured his dating life around them. He looked for instant chemistry and cosmic signs. He made grand gestures when relationships hit rough patches. He avoided addressing problems because he thought true love should be effortless.

When Mark met Jennifer, he was convinced she was "the one" because he felt instant attraction. The fact that she lived in another state, had different career goals, and came from a completely different cultural background didn't matter because love would conquer all.

Mark spent two years in a long-distance relationship, flying back and forth every few weeks, running up credit card debt, and trying to convince Jennifer to move to his city. He made increasingly desperate grand gestures: surprise visits, expensive gifts, elaborate proposals for their future together.

Jennifer ended the relationship because Mark's behavior felt suffocating and his constant pressure to change her life plans showed he didn't respect her autonomy. She'd never asked for grand gestures. She'd wanted a partner who could build something realistic with her instead of someone living in a fantasy.

Mark was devastated because he'd done everything society taught him was romantic and loving. He couldn't understand why his devotion wasn't enough to make the relationship work.

The problem was that Mark confused infatuation with love, drama with passion, and persistence with devotion. Society had taught him that these were the same things, but they're not.

Real love is based on understanding and accepting someone as they are, not projecting fantasies onto them. Real passion comes from genuine compatibility and mutual respect, not from overcoming obstacles and drama. Real devotion means supporting someone's actual goals and happiness, not trying to change their life to fit your vision.

Social media makes societal relationship bullshit worse by creating highlight reels that real couples can't compete with. People post their best moments and most romantic gestures while hiding the daily work that makes relationships function.

Mark started comparing his relationships to what he saw online: perfectly coordinated couple photos, expensive vacations, public declarations of love, and constant displays of happiness. His real relationships felt boring and inadequate compared to the performance he saw on social media.

The dating app culture reinforces other toxic messages. The endless options create the illusion that there's always someone better available. The focus on photos and brief profiles reduces people to commodities to be evaluated and discarded. The gamification of dating turns relationships into competitions instead of connections.

Mark became addicted to the validation of matches and the fantasy of finding someone perfect. Even when he was in relationships, he'd keep checking apps because society taught him that settling was giving up on his dreams.

The self-help relationship industry profits from keeping people confused and hopeful instead of giving them practical skills. Books, seminars, and coaches sell the fantasy that following their system will deliver your perfect relationship instead of teaching the basic communication and boundary skills that make relationships work.

Mark spent thousands of dollars on relationship courses that promised to reveal "the secret" to attracting his ideal woman. None of them taught him how to handle normal relationship conflicts, set healthy boundaries, or recognize compatibility issues early.

Society also promotes toxic ideas about gender roles that make relationships more difficult. Women are taught to expect men to be mind readers who anticipate their needs. Men are taught to expect women to be nurturing mothers who manage their emotions. Both expectations create resentment and disappointment.

Mark expected women to provide constant emotional support and validation while never requiring the same from him. When women had their own problems and needs, he felt burdened and confused. Society had taught him that good women take care of men's feelings, not that relationships require mutual support.

Love requires compatibility. Attraction and feelings aren't enough. You need shared values, compatible life goals, and similar approaches to money, family, and communication.

Relationships require skills. Direct communication, boundary-setting, conflict resolution, and compromise. These can be learned. Most people just never bother.

Work is normal. All healthy relationships require ongoing effort, communication, and adjustment. If it feels effortless, you're probably avoiding important issues.

Consistency matters more than gestures. Daily respect and consideration mean more than occasional grand displays. Show up every day, not just when you need something forgiven.

You can't fix people. Enter relationships with people who are already functional and compatible, not with projects you hope to improve.

Mark eventually learned to ignore society's relationship advice and focus on developing practical relationship skills. He stopped looking for cosmic signs and started paying attention to compatibility and character. He stopped making grand gestures and started providing consistent daily consideration.

He found a relationship that worked when he started treating women as individuals instead of following scripts about what romance should look like. He learned that real love is quieter and more stable than society portrays, but also more satisfying and sustainable.

Society profits from relationship confusion and dysfunction. The entertainment industry needs drama to sell stories. The self-help industry needs problems to sell solutions. Social media needs insecurity to sell products and attention.

None of these industries benefit from teaching you how to build stable, healthy relationships that don't require constant work, products, or entertainment.

Stop consuming society's relationship bullshit and start learning practical skills. Focus on compatibility instead of chemistry. Build relationships gradually instead of expecting instant magic. Address problems directly instead of hoping love will fix them.

Society's version of romance is designed to sell you things, not to help you build lasting connections. Real relationships are less dramatic but more fulfilling than anything you'll see in movies or on social media.

Chapter 22: Digital Age Complications

When Alex saw that his girlfriend Jenny had liked three of her ex-boyfriend's Instagram posts in one day, he felt sick to his stomach. He spent the next hour scrolling through her social media history, checking who she'd been following, and analyzing the timing of her likes and comments. By the time Jenny got home, Alex was convinced she was having an emotional affair.

Jenny thought Alex was being paranoid and controlling. She'd liked a few photos without thinking about it and couldn't understand why Alex was treating it like cheating. But Alex felt like Jenny was publicly flirting with her ex and disrespecting their relationship.

This is the kind of shit that didn't exist twenty years ago. Digital technology has created new ways for relationships to get fucked up that previous generations never had to deal with.

Social media, dating apps, and constant connectivity have introduced complications that most people aren't equipped to handle. Every relationship now must navigate digital boundaries, online temptations, and the performance of happiness for public consumption.

Social media turns every like, comment, follow, and interaction into potential evidence of disloyalty. Partners analyze each other's online activity like forensic investigators looking for signs of cheating or disrespect.

Ex-partners stay permanently visible. Social media makes it nearly impossible to fully disconnect from past relationships. They remain accessible and present, creating ongoing temptation and jealousy that previous generations never had to navigate.

Online emotional affairs develop easily. Text conversations, DMs, and online relationships can become emotionally intense without ever becoming physical. The intimacy of constant digital contact creates bonds that cross lines most people wouldn't cross in person.

Dating app addiction keeps one foot out the door. Even people in relationships sometimes keep apps active for ego validation. The constant possibility of something better makes it harder to commit fully to what's in front of you.

Performance pressure is constant. Social media creates an obligation to present your relationship as perfect and happy. Couples feel they need to post couple photos and romantic gestures to prove their relationship is real and successful.

Constant comparison to curated highlights creates unrealistic expectations. People compare their actual daily reality to other people's best moments, then wonder why their relationship feels inadequate.

Digital surveillance has become normalized. Location tracking, message checking, social media stalking — technology makes monitoring a partner easy, and that ease creates an atmosphere of distrust that poisons even healthy relationships.

Alex and Jenny's Instagram conflict illustrates how social media can turn innocent behavior into relationship problems. Jenny's likes were thoughtless social media habits. Alex's reaction was driven by insecurity and the constant visibility of potential threats.

Neither of them was entirely wrong, but they were both dealing with problems that technology created.

Establish clear social media boundaries early. Discuss what kinds of online interactions you're both comfortable with — be specific about ex-partners, flirtatious comments, and private messaging with people you find attractive.

Stop using social media to investigate your partner. Constantly checking their online activity creates paranoia and corrodes trust. If you feel the need to monitor their behavior, the real problem is either your insecurity or something they've actually done — and neither is fixed by more surveillance.

Keep ex-partners in the past. Unfollow, unfriend, or mute them. Staying connected to past relationships creates unnecessary temptation and jealousy for everyone involved.

Be transparent about online interactions. If someone slides into your DMs or you're having ongoing conversations with attractive people, let your partner know. Secrecy creates suspicion even when nothing inappropriate is happening.

Stop performing your relationship for other people. Focus on being happy together instead of appearing happy to your followers.

Delete dating apps if you're in a committed relationship. There's no good reason to keep them. Having them available creates temptation and sends a clear signal about your level of commitment.

The biggest digital-age complication is that technology makes it easier to avoid dealing with relationship problems directly. Instead of talking to Jenny about his insecurities, Alex used social media surveillance to feed his paranoia. Instead of understanding Alex's concerns, Jenny dismissed them as controlling behavior.

Digital communication also makes it easier to misunderstand each other's intentions. A simple like on Instagram can become evidence of emotional infidelity because online interactions lack context and nuance.

Jenny eventually deleted her ex-boyfriend from social media and adjusted her online behavior to make Alex more comfortable. Alex worked on his insecurity and stopped using social media to monitor Jenny's behavior.

But they both had to learn new relationship skills that previous generations didn't need. They had to navigate digital boundaries, online temptations, and social media jealousy on top of all the normal relationship challenges.

The digital age has made relationships more complicated, but it's also made infidelity and emotional affairs more accessible. The person who might never have cheated physically now has endless opportunities for emotional connections and validation outside their relationship.

None of this means accepting inappropriate behavior or becoming paranoid about technology. It means recognizing that modern relationships require new boundaries and skills that didn't exist before smartphones and social media.

If you're struggling with digital age relationship problems, focus on communication and clear boundaries instead of surveillance and control. Technology should make your relationship easier, not create additional sources of conflict and insecurity.

Chapter 23: Family Dynamics Interference

When Tom introduced his girlfriend Lisa to his mother, everything seemed fine at first. His mom was polite and welcoming during their initial meeting. But within a month, Tom's mother was calling him daily to share concerns about Lisa's "attitude," questioning whether Lisa was "good enough" for him and finding fault with everything from Lisa's job to her appearance to her family background.

Tom felt torn between defending Lisa and maintaining peace with his mother. Lisa felt attacked and unwelcome, but every time she tried to discuss it with Tom, he'd make excuses for his mother's behavior or suggest that Lisa was being too sensitive.

This went on for two years until Tom's mother finally created enough conflict to destroy their relationship. Lisa couldn't handle feeling like she was constantly being judged and criticized by Tom's family, and Tom couldn't handle the stress of managing the conflict between the two most important women in his life.

This is how toxic family dynamics destroy relationships that might otherwise work.

Family interference comes in many forms, but it always involves family members inserting themselves into your relationship in ways that create conflict, undermine your partner, or force you to choose between family loyalty and relationship health.

Undermining your partner is the most common. Family members who consistently criticize, belittle, or find fault plant seeds of doubt about your partner's character, motivations, and suitability. The criticism is usually framed as concern.

Creating loyalty conflicts is the manipulation version. They set up situations where supporting your partner means betraying your family, or vice versa. Every interaction becomes a test of where your real allegiance lies.

Boundary violations look like involvement. They show up uninvited, demand access to private information, or insert themselves into decisions that should be between you and your partner. They call it closeness. It's control.

Financial manipulation is the power version. Money, inheritance, or financial support used as a weapon to control your relationship choices. They threaten to cut you off if you don't comply with their demands about your partner.

Emotional manipulation uses guilt and shame. Claims that you're abandoning the family, forgetting your roots, or being controlled by your partner. The subtext is always that your loyalty to them should outrank everything else.

Triangulation keeps them in the middle. They use other family members to gather information about your relationship, or they share your private relationship information with others. They create communication webs instead of talking to you directly, so they always have more information than you realize.

Tom's mother used several of these tactics. She undermined Lisa through constant criticism and doubt-planting. She created loyalty conflicts by making Tom feel like he had to choose between defending Lisa and maintaining family harmony. She violated boundaries by inserting herself into private relationship matters.

Family interference often comes disguised as love and concern. Tom's mother claimed she was just looking out for his best interests and wanted him to be happy. In reality, she was sabotaging his relationship because she didn't want to share his attention and loyalty.

Lisa eventually realized that she wasn't just dating Tom. She was dealing with his entire family system, and that system was designed to exclude outsiders who might threaten the family's control over Tom.

Set clear boundaries with family members and follow through when they're violated. Make it plain that criticism of your partner is unacceptable. Saying it once without consequences means nothing.

Stop sharing private relationship information with family. Don't give them ammunition by complaining about your partner.

Whatever you share will be used, directly or indirectly, against the relationship.

Present a united front. When family members attack your partner, defend them immediately and clearly. Don't make your partner fight these battles alone or feel like they have to win your family's approval to be safe in your relationship.

Refuse to participate in triangulation. Don't let family members use you to gather information about your partner or relay messages that should be communicated directly. Insist on direct conversation.

Be prepared to limit contact. If family members won't respect your boundaries and continue to interfere, you may need to reduce contact or go no-contact. This isn't abandoning your family. It's protecting what you've chosen to build.

Recognize when guilt, financial pressure, or emotional blackmail are being used to control your relationship choices. Your happiness and your partnership should take priority over family approval. That's not selfish. That's adulthood.

The hardest part about dealing with family interference is accepting that your family might not want what's best for you. They might want what's best for them, what maintains their control, or what fits their vision of your life.

Tom struggled with this reality because he'd been taught that family always comes first and that good sons prioritize their mothers' feelings. He couldn't see that his mother's "concern" was about maintaining her position as the most important woman in his life.

Family interference is damaging because it attacks the foundation of trust and partnership that healthy relationships require. When your family consistently undermines your partner, it creates an atmosphere where your partner feels unsafe and unsupported.

Lisa couldn't build a secure relationship with Tom when she knew his family was constantly working against her and that Tom might side with them over her in conflicts. She needed to know that Tom would protect and defend their relationship against external threats, including his own family.

Some families genuinely have your best interests at heart and will support healthy relationships even if they have initial concerns. But toxic families will continue to interfere and undermine regardless of how good your partner is or how happy your relationship makes you.

The difference is whether family members will respect your boundaries and accept your choices, or whether they continue to fight for control over your life and relationships.

If your family consistently interferes with your relationships, creates loyalty conflicts, or refuses to respect your boundaries, you're dealing with toxic family dynamics that will destroy any relationship you try to build until you address them directly.

Chapter 24: Recovery After Toxic Relationships

After Jake finally left his manipulative ex-girlfriend Rachel, he thought the hard part was over. He was wrong. Six months later, Jake was still jumping every time his phone buzzed, analyzing every interaction with new women for signs of manipulation, and second-guessing his own perceptions about normal relationship behavior.

When Jake started dating again, he found himself either running away from perfectly healthy women because they reminded him of Rachel in some small way, or gravitating toward women who displayed familiar toxic patterns because that felt "normal" to him.

Jake's judgment about relationships was completely fucked up, and he didn't even realize it.

This happens after toxic relationships. They don't just end when you leave. They rewire your brain, damage your ability to trust your own perceptions, and create patterns that can sabotage future relationships if you don't address them directly.

Recovery from toxic relationships isn't just about healing from what happened. It's about rebuilding your ability to recognize healthy behavior, trust your own judgment, and form secure connections with people who aren't trying to manipulate or control you.

Hypervigilance hits first. After being manipulated and lied to, you become hypersensitive to potential threats. Every small inconsistency or moment of emotional distance feels like evidence that your new partner is hiding something or preparing to hurt you.

Healthy behavior starts to feel suspicious. Toxic relationships normalize dysfunction. When someone treats you with basic respect and consideration, it can feel foreign or too good to be true. You might interpret healthy boundaries as rejection or genuine kindness as manipulation.

Trauma bonding creates a withdrawal effect. Toxic relationships create intense emotional highs and lows that become addictive. Healthy relationships can feel boring by comparison because they don't provide the same adrenaline. Your nervous system has been calibrated to chaos.

Self-doubt lingers. Gaslighting and manipulation damage your confidence in your own perceptions. You second-guess your feelings, memories, and reactions because you've been trained to distrust yourself.

Toxic patterns repeat without conscious intervention. You might find yourself attracted to familiar types of people or recreating familiar dynamics, even when you know they're unhealthy. It feels like home even when it's a disaster.

Vulnerability becomes terrifying. Being hurt in a toxic relationship makes it genuinely frightening to open up to new people. You might keep potential partners at arm's length to protect yourself, then wonder why nothing develops.

Jake experienced all of these challenges. He was attracted to women who were emotionally unavailable because that felt familiar. When he met women who were genuinely interested in him and treated him well, he felt uncomfortable and suspicious of their motives.

He also recreated some of the toxic dynamics from his relationship with Rachel. He'd test new partners to see if they would manipulate him, create conflict to see how they'd react, or withdraw emotionally to protect himself from potential hurt.

Get professional help. Toxic relationships cause real psychological damage that often requires therapy to address. A good therapist can help you process what happened, rebuild self-trust, and learn to recognize healthy patterns before they feel foreign.

Take time before dating again. Don't jump straight into something new. You need time to heal, rebuild your sense of self, and develop the ability to recognize and maintain healthy connections before you bring someone else into the wreckage.

Study what healthy actually looks like. Read about secure attachment and respectful conflict resolution. You need new models to replace the toxic ones you internalized. If chaos is your baseline, stability will feel wrong until you rewire it.

Start trusting your perceptions in low-stakes situations. Rebuild confidence in your own judgment gradually. Trust your instincts about non-romantic situations first, then extend that trust to how you read people.

Identify your triggers and patterns. Understand what behaviors or types of people activate your trauma responses. Develop strategies to recognize them without letting them drive your decisions.

Practice boundary-setting in all your relationships, not just romantic ones. Learn to say no, express your needs, and protect your emotional wellbeing without feeling guilty for it.

Build a support network of healthy people who can help you reality-check when your trauma responses might be distorting your judgment.

Jake eventually realized that his idea of what relationships should feel like was completely distorted by his experience with Rachel. He thought relationships were supposed to be intense, dramatic, and emotionally volatile because that's what he'd experienced.

Learning that healthy relationships could be stable, peaceful, and secure without being boring was a revelation for him. He had to consciously choose to invest in and trust relationships that felt "different" from what he was used to.

The recovery process also involves grieving the time and energy you lost to toxic relationships and accepting that you might have trust issues that take time to resolve. This isn't a personal failing. It's a normal response to psychological abuse.

Jake had to accept that his trust issues resulted from being systematically lied to and manipulated, not evidence that he was broken or unable to have healthy relationships. Understanding this helped him be patient with his own healing process.

Recovery from toxic relationships is possible, but it requires conscious effort and often professional support. Without addressing the damage these relationships cause, you're likely to either avoid healthy relationships out of fear or repeat toxic patterns because they feel familiar.

The goal isn't to become someone who never gets hurt or never makes relationship mistakes. The goal is to rebuild your ability to trust your own judgment, recognize healthy behavior, and form secure connections with people who enhance your life instead of damaging it.

If you're struggling to trust again, feeling paranoid in new relationships, or finding yourself attracted to familiar toxic patterns, these are signs you need to focus on recovery before pursuing new romantic connections. Healing isn't giving up on love. It's preparing yourself to recognize and maintain the kind of love that's worth having.

Chapter 25: What to Do When Your Partner Gaslights You

When David confronted his girlfriend Emma about flirting with her coworker at their company party, Emma told him he was being paranoid and jealous. When he pointed out specific things he'd witnessed, she said he was misremembering what happened. When he mentioned that other people at the party had noticed her behavior too, she said he was turning people against her and creating drama.

By the end of the conversation, David was questioning his own perceptions and apologizing for bringing it up. Emma had successfully convinced him that his legitimate concerns were character defects on his part.

This is gaslighting, and it's one of the most destructive forms of psychological manipulation in relationships.

Gaslighting is when someone systematically makes you question your own memory, perceptions, and sanity. They deny things that happened, rewrite history to benefit themselves, and convince you that your legitimate concerns are signs that something's wrong with you.

The term comes from a 1944 movie where a husband dims the gaslights in their house and then denies that the lights are flickering when his wife notices. He makes her think she's going crazy so he can control her.

Modern gaslighting works the same way. Your partner does or says something fucked up, you call them out on it, and they convince you that you're the problem for noticing or caring about their behavior.

Emma wasn't just denying that she flirted with her coworker. She was attacking David's ability to trust his own observations. She made him feel like his perceptions were unreliable and his emotions were inappropriate.

This is psychological warfare designed to break down your confidence in your own judgment so you become dependent on the gaslighter's version of reality.

Flat denial. They tell you it never happened. When you bring up something they said or did, they act like you're making it up or imagining things. The goal is to make you distrust your own memory.

Sensitivity dismissal. "You're being too sensitive." They frame your reactions as overreactions. Everything that bothers you becomes evidence that you're emotionally unstable or dramatic.

Version replacement. "You're remembering it wrong." They acknowledge something happened but claim your version is inaccurate. They provide an alternative explanation that makes their behavior innocent and your concerns unreasonable.

Identity attacks. "You're crazy. You're paranoid. You're jealous." Instead of addressing your concerns, they suggest the real problem is your psychological instability. This shifts the conversation from their behavior to your mental state.

Social proof claims. "Everyone thinks you're being ridiculous." They invoke other people's supposed agreement to isolate you and make you feel like the entire world sees you as the problem.

Gaslighting works gradually. Each individual incident might seem minor, but over time it erodes your confidence in your own perceptions until you start automatically doubting yourself instead of trusting your observations.

David knew what he saw at the party, but Emma's response made him question whether he was being reasonable. After months of similar incidents, David stopped trusting his own judgment and started accepting Emma's version of events even when it contradicted his direct experience.

Trust your initial perceptions. Your first instinct about what happened is usually accurate. Don't let anyone talk you out of what you clearly observed or experienced.

Document incidents immediately. Write down what happened as soon as possible — specific details, dates, witnesses. This prevents the gaslighter from rewriting history later and keeps you anchored to what actually occurred.

Don't argue about reality. When someone denies something that obviously happened, don't try to convince them. Say "I know what I experienced" and end the conversation. You're not required to justify your perceptions to someone who's attacking them.

Get outside perspectives. Talk to trusted friends or family about what's happening. Gaslighters work to isolate you from other viewpoints, so maintaining connections with people who validate your reality is crucial to staying grounded.

End conversations that become reality disputes. When someone tries to gaslight you, remove yourself immediately. Don't reward it with continued engagement or lengthy argument. Just stop.

Consider whether this relationship is salvageable at all. People who gaslight are fundamentally disrespecting your ability to understand your own experience. This isn't a communication problem. It's psychological abuse.

The hardest part about dealing with gaslighting is accepting that someone you care about is deliberately trying to undermine your sanity. Most people want to believe their partner's manipulation is unintentional or that they can reason with them.

This is usually a mistake. Gaslighting requires a deliberate effort to deny reality and attack someone's perceptions. People who do this know exactly what they're doing, and they're doing it because it works.

David eventually realized that Emma's pattern of denying his reality wasn't about poor communication or different perspectives. It was about control. She wanted to do whatever she wanted without being held accountable, so she trained him to stop trusting his own observations.

Once he understood this, David stopped trying to convince Emma to acknowledge reality and started focusing on protecting his own mental health. He documented her gaslighting attempts, stopped engaging in arguments about what happened, and eventually ended the relationship.

If your partner regularly makes you question your own sanity, memory, or perceptions, you're not in a healthy relationship. You're being psychologically abused, and no amount of better communication will fix someone who's intentionally trying to break down your grip on reality.

Chapter 26: When Your Partner Is a Narcissist

Rob's girlfriend Maria had two completely different personalities depending on who was watching. In public, she was charming, helpful, and seemed genuinely interested in other people. She'd volunteer for charity events, remember everyone's birthdays, and always knew exactly what to say to make people feel special.

In private, Maria was a different person entirely. She'd rage at Rob for minor infractions, demand constant praise and attention, and punish him with the silent treatment when he didn't meet her expectations. She'd criticize his appearance, his job, his friends, and his family, but if he ever pointed out her behavior, she'd either explode in anger or break down crying about how mean he was being to her.

Rob spent two years thinking he was dating someone with mood swings before he realized he was dating a narcissist.

Narcissistic personality disorder affects how someone relates to other people and sees themselves. Narcissists have an inflated sense of their own importance, a desperate need for admiration, and a complete lack of empathy for others. They see relationships as transactions where other people exist to serve their needs.

There are two main types of narcissists, and both will fuck up your life in different ways.

Overt narcissists are the obvious ones. They're grandiose, attention-seeking, and openly believe they're superior to everyone around them. They brag constantly, demand to be the center of attention, and throw tantrums when they don't get their way. They're easy to spot because they make everything about themselves in obvious ways.

Covert narcissists are the dangerous ones because they're harder to recognize. They present themselves as victims, martyrs, or misunderstood geniuses. They get their narcissistic supply through manipulation, passive-aggression, and playing victim when called out on their behavior.

Maria was a covert narcissist. She maintained her public image by appearing selfless and caring but used that reputation to manipulate people into giving her attention and sympathy. When Rob called out her private behavior, she'd twist it into evidence that he was abusive and she was the victim.

They can't handle criticism or accountability. Any attempt to address their behavior results in rage, tears, deflection, or attacking you instead. They never take responsibility and always find ways to make themselves the victim in their own story.

They lack genuine empathy. They might perform empathy when it benefits them, but they don't actually care about your feelings or experiences. Your emotions only matter to them when they affect their own comfort or image.

Everything has to revolve around them. Your achievements get minimized, your problems get ignored, and conversations always end up being about them somehow. They need constant validation and attention to function.

They believe they're special. They expect treatment that matches their inflated self-image and get angry when they don't receive it. They often claim to be victims of jealousy or misunderstanding when people push back.

They exploit relationships. They use people to get what they want and discard them when they're no longer useful. They keep backup sources of attention and validation in case their primary source leaves or wises up.

They rewrite history to benefit themselves. They'll deny things that happened, change details to make themselves look better, and gaslight you about your own experiences and memories. This is how they maintain their narrative.

Living with a narcissist is exhausting because you're constantly walking on eggshells, managing their emotions, and having your reality questioned. They train you to prioritize their needs over your own through a combination of intermittent reinforcement, emotional manipulation, and psychological abuse.

Rob noticed that he'd stopped expressing opinions that might upset Maria, stopped spending time with friends she didn't like, and started monitoring his own behavior constantly to avoid triggering her rage or tears. He'd become so focused on managing her reactions that he'd lost touch with his own needs and feelings.

This is exactly what narcissists want. They need you to be completely focused on them and their emotional state. Your job becomes managing their ego and providing them with the validation they crave.

Don't try to fix them or help them see their behavior. Narcissists don't want to change because they don't think anything is wrong with them. Trying to make them understand how their behavior affects you is pointless and will only give them more material to use against you.

Document their behavior. Keep records of incidents, especially when they deny things that happened or try to rewrite history. Narcissists are skilled at making you question your own memory, and documentation keeps you anchored to reality.

Maintain your connections with supportive people. Narcissists work to isolate you from friends and family who might validate your reality or encourage you to leave. Don't let them cut you off from the people who know you.

Set and enforce boundaries without negotiation. Don't reward their tantrums with attention or compliance. When they cross your boundaries, follow through with consequences immediately.

Don't take their behavior personally. Narcissists treat everyone badly eventually. Their abuse isn't about you being inadequate. It's about them being fundamentally incapable of healthy relationships.

Start planning your exit strategy now. Most relationships with narcissists don't improve over time — they get worse as the narcissist becomes more comfortable showing who they are. The sooner you plan, the more of yourself you'll have left when you go.

The hardest part about leaving a narcissist is accepting that the person you fell in love with wasn't real. The charming, caring person they showed you in the beginning was a performance designed to hook you. The cruel, selfish person they become is who they truly are.

Rob kept hoping Maria would go back to being the person she was when they first met. He didn't understand that she'd never been that person. She'd been performing a role to capture his attention and investment. Once she felt secure in the relationship, she dropped the act and showed him who she really was.

Narcissists don't get better with love, patience, or understanding. They get worse because they interpret your tolerance as permission to escalate their abuse. The only way to win with a narcissist is not to play their game.

If you recognize these patterns in your relationship, start planning your exit now. Don't wait for them to change or hope that you can love them into being a better person. Protect yourself and get out while you still remember who you are.

Chapter 27: When to Walk Away

Sometimes the best relationship skill is knowing when to quit. Not every relationship problem can be solved with better communication or understanding different patterns. Some relationships are genuinely toxic, and the healthiest thing you can do is get the fuck out.

The problem is that most people stay too long in relationships that are damaging them. They think if they just try harder, communicate better, or be more understanding, they can fix whatever's wrong. They confuse persistence with wisdom and endurance with strength.

This is bullshit. Sometimes the smart move is to walk away, and recognizing when you've reached that point can save you years of misery.

Here are the signs that tell you it's time to go:

Physical violence or threats of violence. No acceptable level exists. If someone puts their hands on you in anger, you leave. Not after a conversation, not after they apologize, not after they promise it won't happen again. You leave.

Patterns of manipulation and emotional abuse. When someone consistently lies to you, gaslights you, threatens self-harm to control your behavior, or systematically destroys your self-esteem, you're not in a relationship. You're in an abusive situation. No amount of communication will fix someone who enjoys controlling and hurting you.

Active addiction they refuse to address. You can't have a healthy relationship with someone whose addiction takes priority over everything else in their life. If they won't get help or admit they have a problem, you can't fix them by staying.

Consistent infidelity. If someone cheats on you repeatedly, they've shown you who they are. One mistake might be forgivable if they take full responsibility and do the actual work. A pattern of cheating means they don't respect you or the relationship.

Financial abuse or exploitation. Stealing from you, running up debt in your name, preventing you from working, using money to control your behavior — this is abuse, and it only escalates over time.

Fundamental incompatibility on deal-breaker issues. If you want kids and they don't, if your values and life goals are completely opposed, no amount of compromise will bridge that gap. Stop wasting time trying to change each other's minds about things neither of you can compromise on.

Mental illness they refuse to treat. You can support someone who is actively working to get help. You cannot save someone who refuses to acknowledge their problems. Their untreated illness becomes your prison if you stay.

They consistently violate boundaries you've clearly stated. If you've communicated your limits clearly and they keep crossing them anyway, they're telling you your boundaries don't matter to them. That won't improve with more communication. It will get worse.

The hardest part about walking away is accepting that some people can't or won't change, no matter how much you love them or how hard you try to help them.

You might see their potential. You might remember who they used to be. You might hope they'll get their shit together eventually.

None of that matters if they're not actively working to change right now.

Love isn't enough to sustain a relationship. You also need respect, compatibility, shared values, and basic emotional safety. When those things are absent, love becomes a trap that keeps you in a situation that's damaging your mental health and wasting your time.

Walking away doesn't make you weak, selfish, or a quitter. It makes you someone who values their own wellbeing enough to leave situations that are harming them.

The people who guilt you for setting boundaries or leaving toxic relationships are usually people who benefit from your dysfunction or who are trapped in their own unhealthy situations and want company.

Don't listen to them. Listen to your gut, your friends who care about your wellbeing, and the evidence of how this person treats you instead of their promises about how they'll treat you in the future.

Some relationships are fixable with better communication and understanding. Others are broken and will only damage you if you stay. Learning to tell the difference will save you years of pain and help you find relationships that add value to your life instead of draining it.

You deserve relationships that improve your life, not ones that make it worse. Don't settle for less because you're afraid of being alone or because you think you can fix someone who doesn't want to be fixed.

Chapter 28: Be Your Authentic Self

After everything in this book, you might think relationships are impossibly complicated. They're not. Most of the bullshit in this book happens because people aren't being authentic and because they refuse to do the basic work that relationships require.

The solution isn't learning to manipulate people better or memorizing scripts for every situation. The solution is being genuinely yourself while developing the skills to communicate and compromise with other genuine people.

This sounds simple, but it's not easy. Most people have been performing for so long that they've forgotten who they are underneath the act. They've been told to be what others want instead of being themselves and finding people who appreciate their authentic personality.

Being authentic doesn't mean being selfish, inconsiderate, or refusing to grow. It means being honest about who you are, what you need, and what you're willing to give in relationships. It means expressing your genuine thoughts and feelings instead of saying what you think others want to hear.

Tim spent most of his twenties trying to be the perfect boyfriend for every woman he dated. With Sarah, he pretended to love hiking even though he hated being outdoors. With Michelle, he acted like he wanted kids immediately even though he wasn't ready. With Amanda, he suppressed his sense of humor because she found it immature.

None of these relationships lasted because Tim was exhausting himself maintaining performances that had nothing to do with who he was. The women weren't falling in love with Tim. They were falling in love with characters he was playing, and he couldn't keep up the act forever.

When Tim finally started being himself—a guy who preferred indoor activities, wasn't ready for kids, and had a slightly juvenile sense of humor—he worried that women wouldn't find him interesting. Instead, he found that the women who liked his authentic self were much better matches than the ones who'd been attracted to his performances.

Authenticity attracts the right people and repels the wrong ones. This is a feature, not a bug. You want to filter out people who aren't compatible with who you are. Pretending to be someone else just delays the inevitable incompatibility discovery and wastes everyone's time.

But being authentic isn't enough by itself. Relationships also require communication skills that most people never learn because they assume love should make everything automatic.

Real communication means saying what you mean clearly and directly. It means listening to understand instead of listening to defend or argue. It means asking for what you need instead of hoping the other person will figure it out. It means addressing problems when they're small instead of letting them build into relationship-ending conflicts.

Tim had to learn that being authentic included being authentically communicative. He couldn't just be himself and expect everything to work out. He had to express his authentic thoughts and needs in ways that other people could understand and respond to.

When Tim's girlfriend Lisa started making comments about moving in together after three months of dating, his authentic feeling was that it was too soon. Instead of hinting that he wasn't ready or avoiding the conversation, he said directly, "I'm enjoying our relationship, but three months feels too early for me to move in together. Can we revisit this in a few months?"

Lisa appreciated his honesty even though she was initially disappointed. They were able to discuss their different timelines and find a compromise that worked for both of them. The conversation strengthened their relationship because it was based on authentic communication instead of assumptions and avoidance.

Relationships also require compromise, which means both people adjusting their preferences to accommodate each other without losing themselves in the process. Compromise isn't about one person always giving in or about meeting exactly in the middle on every issue. It's about finding solutions that respect both people's core needs.

Tim loved action movies and Lisa preferred romantic comedies. Instead of fighting about what to watch or one person always sacrificing for the other, they alternated movie choices and sometimes watched different things on their own. They also discovered they both enjoyed crime dramas, which became their go-to genre for watching together.

Effective compromise requires both people to distinguish between preferences and deal-breakers. Tim could compromise on movie choices because his preference for action films wasn't a core need. But he couldn't compromise on having kids because Lisa wanted them and he didn't. That incompatibility eventually ended their relationship, and that was the right outcome for both of them.

The key to successful compromise is maintaining your authentic self while adapting your behaviors and preferences where possible. You can change what you watch, where you eat, and how you spend weekends without changing who you fundamentally are as a person.

Tim learned that authentic compromise felt different from the fake accommodation he'd done in previous relationships. When he pretended to love hiking with Sarah, he was betraying his authentic self to avoid conflict. When he alternated movie choices with Lisa, he was maintaining his authentic preferences while accommodating hers.

Authentic relationships require both people to show up as themselves and do the work necessary to build something together. This means communicating clearly, compromising fairly, and addressing conflicts directly instead of hoping they'll disappear.

Most relationship problems can be solved when both people are willing to be honest about what they need and work together to find solutions. The patterns in this book become destructive when people avoid authenticity and refuse to do relationship work.

The selective equality trap happens when people aren't honest about what gestures mean to them and refuse to communicate their emotional needs clearly. The hint and hope pattern happens when people avoid direct communication and expect mind-reading instead of clarity.

Sexual frequency conflicts happen when people aren't authentic about their actual desires and refuse to compromise on meeting each other's needs. Emotional labor imbalances happen when people aren't honest about their capabilities and refuse to negotiate fair distribution of relationship work.

Most of the toxic behaviors in this book are attempts to get needs met without being vulnerable enough to ask for them directly. Manipulation is what happens when people want something but are too afraid or too entitled to communicate and compromise authentically.

Being your authentic self in relationships means accepting that you can't control other people's responses to you. Some people won't like your genuine personality, and that's fine. You're not trying to be universally appealing. You're trying to find people who appreciate who you are.

Tim discovered that authentic relationships felt completely different from his previous performances. There was less drama because there were no false expectations to maintain. There was less anxiety because he wasn't constantly wondering if his act was convincing. There was more intimacy because people were connecting with his real self instead of his persona.

Authentic relationships also handle conflict better because both people are invested in solving problems instead of protecting images. When Tim and his current girlfriend disagree about something, they focus on finding solutions that work for both of them instead of defending their positions or avoiding the conversation.

Being authentic doesn't guarantee relationship success. You might be genuinely incompatible with someone, and no amount of communication and compromise will bridge fundamental differences in values, life goals, or personality. But authenticity ensures that if a relationship fails, it fails for real reasons instead of because of misunderstandings or false advertising.

Tim's relationship with Lisa ended because they had incompatible life goals, not because of communication problems or unaddressed patterns. They were both sad about the breakup, but they respected each other's honesty and remained friends. The relationship didn't work, but it didn't damage either of them.

This is what healthy relationship endings look like when people are authentic and communicative. Sometimes incompatibilities can't be compromised away, and that's information worth having instead of spending years trying to force something that doesn't fit.

The alternative to authenticity is spending your life maintaining performances for people who don't know you. The alternative to communication and compromise is relationships full of unaddressed conflicts and unmet needs. Neither alternative leads to the kind of connections that make life better.

Start with yourself. Figure out who you are when you're not performing for others. Identify your core values, genuine interests, and non-negotiable needs. Develop the confidence to express these authentically instead of hiding them to be more appealing.

Then learn the skills necessary to build relationships with other authentic people. Practice direct communication. Learn to compromise without losing yourself. Develop the ability to address conflicts constructively instead of avoiding them or escalating them.

These skills take practice, but they're not complicated. Most relationship problems have simple solutions when both people are willing to be honest and work together. The complexity comes from all the bullshit people add to avoid doing the basic work.

Be yourself. Say what you mean. Listen to understand. Ask for what you need. Compromise where possible. Address problems directly. These principles will serve you better than any manipulation technique or relationship strategy.

The goal isn't to find someone who completes you or to become someone who deserves love. The goal is to be a complete person who can build something meaningful with another complete person. That's how real relationships work, and it's worth the effort it requires.

Stop believing the bullshit that makes relationships harder than they need to be. Ignore society's fairy tale romance myths. Reject the toxic advice your parents passed down. Forget the manipulation tactics and gender war strategies that turn people into enemies instead of partners.

Relationships are simple when you strip away all the crap that doesn't work. Be yourself. Find someone who likes who you are. Communicate directly. Compromise fairly. Address problems honestly.

That's it. No complicated systems, no performance strategies, no mind games. Just two people choosing to build something real together.

Get rid of the bullshit, and focus on what works.

Conclusion

Women are not the enemy. I want to be clear about that before you close this book.

Everything in these pages — the patterns, the manipulation tactics, the exit strategies — none of it is about building a case against women. It's about understanding what's actually happening so you can stop reacting and start choosing.

Most men walk into relationships on autopilot. They're running programs installed by their fathers, their mothers, their friends, the internet, the red pill, the blue pill, pickup artists, feminists, and every other voice that had an opinion about how men should behave with women. They don't know why they do what they do. They just do it, it blows up, and they blame her.

That's not a relationship. That's a pattern repeating itself.

The shift this book is asking you to make is from reactive to intentional. You can decide what kind of man you want to be in relationships. You can decide what you'll accept and what you won't. You can decide when to invest and when to walk. None of that requires a system, a community, or a guru. It requires you to think clearly about what you actually want and stop letting other people's noise make that decision for you.

One specific thing worth saying directly: don't walk into a relationship focused on sex. Not because desire is wrong — it's not — but because leading with it tells a woman everything about where you rank her. Build something first. That might take a few dates or a few months depending on the person and the situation. Let it develop. Women know what you're there for regardless, but they also know whether you see them as a person or a destination. The difference in how you're treated will reflect exactly which one you communicated.

And for the love of God, don't be a pushover. Women don't want that and they don't respect it. You will get friendzoned so fast your head will spin. Be masculine. Be direct. Have opinions and hold them. Handle your own problems. Show up as a man, not as someone auditioning to be liked.

At the same time — and this is the whole point — remember that she's a person. A complete, complicated, differently-wired person who processes the world in ways you don't. You're going to think differently. You're going to want different things at different times. You're going to misread each other constantly until you stop assuming your way is the only way.

That's not a problem to solve. That's just what it is.

The men who have the best relationships aren't the ones who figured out women. They're the ones who figured out themselves, stopped performing, and found someone worth being real with.

That's available to you. It's not complicated. It's just not easy.

Choose wisely.

Glossary of Relationship Terms

Amused Mastery — Red pill term for staying detached and entertained when a woman tries to get a reaction out of you. The idea is that nothing she does can shake your frame. In practice it's just trained emotional unavailability with a better name.

Boundary Violation — When someone crosses a limit you've clearly stated, more than once, after they knew exactly where the line was. One mistake is a mistake. Repeated violations are information about how much they respect you.

Covert Narcissist — The dangerous kind. Unlike overt narcissists who are obviously full of themselves, covert narcissists play the victim, the martyr, the misunderstood genius. They get what they need through manipulation and passive aggression. Harder to spot, just as destructive.

Dread Game — Red pill tactic where you keep your partner off-balance by implying you might leave or that other women want you. It's relationship management through manufactured insecurity. Works short-term on the wrong women, and tells you everything about what kind of relationship you're building.

Emotional Blackmail — Using threats of self-harm, suicide, or emotional breakdown to prevent someone from leaving or setting a limit. The person doing it has figured out that your concern for their wellbeing can be turned into a control mechanism. Treat the threat seriously. Don't reward it with compliance.

Emotional Labor — The work of maintaining relationships — noticing when something's wrong, starting hard conversations, managing the emotional temperature, remembering what matters to people. It's real work. When one person does all of it and the other just shows up, that's an imbalance that will eventually implode.

False Fragility — Acting helpless or incompetent to avoid responsibility or get someone else to do things for you. It's not weakness — it's a strategy. The person doing it is usually quite capable when there's something in it for them.

Frame Control — Red pill concept about controlling how situations get interpreted. Whoever defines the reality of an interaction has the power. Not entirely wrong as an observation. Completely exhausting as a way to live.

Gaslighting — Making someone question their own memory, perceptions, and sanity by denying things that happened, rewriting history, and convincing them that their legitimate concerns are signs of psychological instability. It's not a communication problem. It's psychological abuse.

Hint and Hope Pattern — Dropping indirect signals about what you want instead of asking directly, then getting upset when the other person doesn't pick up on them. Women do this more than men because direct requests feel demanding. Men miss the hints because they process communication literally. Nobody wins.

Intermittent Reinforcement — Unpredictable cycles of reward and punishment that create psychological dependency. Same mechanism as a slot machine. When someone is sometimes wonderful and sometimes awful with no pattern you can predict, your brain gets hooked trying to figure it out. Explains why toxic relationships are hard to leave.

Love Bombing — Overwhelming someone with attention, affection, gifts, and future promises in the early stages of a relationship. It feels like intense chemistry. It's actually about creating emotional dependency before the person has had time to see who you really are. When someone moves this fast, slow down deliberately and watch what happens.

Overt Narcissist — The obvious kind — grandiose, attention-seeking, openly superior. Easy to spot because they make everything about themselves without trying to hide it. Still destructive, just less sneaky about it than the covert variety.

Passive-Aggressive Communication — Expressing anger, frustration, or resentment indirectly — through silence, coldness, sarcasm, or doing things badly on purpose — instead of just saying what's wrong. Creates conflict without ever owning it. The other person ends up frustrated and confused while the passive-aggressive person plays innocent.

Pattern-Proof Skills — Communication and boundary techniques that work regardless of who you're dealing with — direct communication, boundary setting, emotional regulation, reality testing, flexible problem-solving. You don't need to diagnose every personality type. You just need skills that hold up under pressure.

Reality Testing — Checking your own perceptions against actual evidence and trusted outside perspectives instead of accepting someone else's version of events. Essential when dealing with gaslighters and manipulators who need you to distrust yourself.

Red Pill — An online ideology claiming to reveal the harsh truth about female nature and sexual dynamics. Takes some real observations about confidence and attraction and turns them into a worldview where relationships are war. The techniques work on the wrong women. The mindset makes genuine connection impossible.

Sexual Coercion — Pressuring someone into sexual activity through guilt, manipulation, wearing them down, or framing their reluctance as a relationship problem. Doesn't require physical force. The answer to hesitation is backing off, not finding new angles.

Shit Test — Red pill term for when a woman challenges, provokes, or tests a man's confidence or reaction. Sometimes it's a real test. Sometimes she's just having a bad day. The red pill answer is to stay amused and unaffected. The human answer is to respond like a person.

Simp — Derogatory term for a man who is excessively accommodating, submissive, or desperate for female approval. Overused as an insult by men who confuse being a decent person with being a doormat. There's a real thing being pointed at here — men who abandon their own needs and self-respect to please women — but the word gets thrown at any man who isn't performing dominance.

Social Manipulation — Using gossip, reputation threats, or group dynamics to control someone's behavior. Getting to mutual friends first with your version of events. Threatening to tell people you're abusive if they don't comply. Playing the social environment instead of dealing with the person directly.

Toxic Femininity — When traditionally feminine traits — emotional sensitivity, vulnerability, social connection — get weaponized to control others and avoid accountability. Tears that shut down conversations. Victim positioning that deflects responsibility. Not what most women do. Common enough that men need to recognize it.

Toxic Masculinity — When traditionally masculine traits — aggression, dominance, emotional suppression — get expressed in ways that damage relationships and the men themselves. The problem isn't masculinity. The problem is specific expressions of it that substitute control for connection.

Trauma Bonding — The psychological attachment that forms between abuser and victim through cycles of abuse followed by affection. The highs and lows create the same kind of dependency as addiction. Explains why people stay in relationships that are clearly hurting them and why leaving feels impossible even when they know they should.

Triangulation — Dragging third parties into conflicts or communication that should be handled directly. Using other family members to gather information. Going to mutual friends instead of the person you have a problem with. Creates drama, erodes trust, and ensures nothing actually gets resolved.

Weaponizing Emotions — Using tears, breakdowns, or claims of being triggered as tools to shut down conversations, avoid accountability, or get what you want. Distinguishable from genuine emotional responses by the timing — it tends to happen exactly when accountability is about to arrive.

About the Author

Richard Lowe has published 113 books and ghostwritten more than 53 of them. He's been a Director of Computer Operations, a Vice President at two consulting firms, a professional photographer who documented over 1,200 belly dance shows and 300 Renaissance festivals, and a widower who spent twelve and a half years in a marriage that taught him everything about what not to do in a relationship.

He doesn't have much patience for people who think the truth should be softened for comfort. That's not a political position. It's a personality trait forged from decades of learning things the hard way.

He spent eight years immersed in the belly dance and performance world, surrounded by hundreds of women every weekend, learning how to be a genuine friend to women without any agenda attached. He sponsored shows that donated proceeds to domestic abuse shelters. He once had 200 belly dancers perform at his birthday party. He photographed mermaids, Renaissance reenactors, WWE wrestlers, and the first world mermaid beauty pageant. His life has not been boring.

He has ghostwritten books for celebrities, tech executives, coaches, and people with stories the world needed to hear but who couldn't find the words themselves. He has appeared on 100+ podcasts. He has helped people who had never written a word produce books that changed their careers and in some cases their lives.

This book is his. Not a client's. His own voice, his own experience, his own conclusions drawn from thirty-plus years of doing it wrong, doing it right, and watching other people do both.

He writes at masterofworlds.com. His ghostwriting practice is at thewritingking.com.

Books by Richard Lowe

See books by Richard Lowe at

https://masterofworlds.com

Get free publishing insights and industry updates at

https://thewritingking.substack.com

For ghostwriting and book coaching services see

https://thewritingking.com